The
NEWLYWED
HANDBOOK

The NEWLYWED HANDBOOK

A Refreshing, Practical Guide for Living Together

Yvonne Garrett

WORD BOOKS
PUBLISHER
WACO, TEXAS

ISBN 0–8499–2931–8
Library of Congress catalog card number: 80–53255
Printed in the United States of America

With Love
To Vernon
who, though he thought a book
could be written in a week,
gave me
six months.

CONTENTS

Acknowledgments	9
Preface	11
Introduction	13
1. INDIVIDUAL IDENTITIES	17
2. EMOTIONAL AND PERSONALITY DIFFERENCES	28
3. INTIMACY	38
4. LIKING YOURSELF	48
5. IN-LAWS AND FAMILY	57
6. COMMUNICATION	69
7. FIGHTING	79
8. MONEY	90
9. TIME	102
10. FRIENDS	113
11. HAVING FUN	123
12. FAMILY RITUALS	137
Notes	153

ACKNOWLEDGMENTS

I must begin with Ruby and Gordon Hill, Adult Bible Study leaders, who ten years ago asked me to help initiate a class in *Marriage and the Family*. No appropriate material being available to us, Gene Vickrey, Minister of Pastoral Care at South Main Baptist Church, helped design the curriculum; he and George Thompson, Marriage and Family Counselor, lent advice and helped with numerous sessions. Bob Hines, Minister of Adult Education, instigated the idea of putting the material into publication form. Floyd Thatcher, Executive Editor and Vice President of Word Books, and Joey Paul, Editorial Director for the Educational Products Division, gave invaluable suggestions. Pat Wienandt polished my manuscript and became my friend. A special thanks goes to my associate Bill Wylie who, along with his wife Susan, finds joy in entertaining and befriending those who come through our classes. Kenneth and Barbara Chafin inspired and encouraged.

I am indebted to members who shared experiences, clipped articles, brought magazines (and even two letters from mothers!), called to say, "I just heard—" or to remind me to watch a TV show pertaining to marriage.

Thanks go to my brother Harry, who for years has

asked, "When are you going to write a book?," to friends who kept me on my toes by inquiring about my progress, and, of course, to my family who made it possible for me to hide away and write.

And thanks especially to those who prayed for me and my book.

PREFACE

When I sat down to read Yvonne Garrett's manuscript I had expected a good book because of what I knew about the author. Over almost a decade I've watched her function as a wife and mother, and for several years I've seen the effect her class in marriage has had for the young couples who were lucky enough to make the limited enrollment. But since it is a first book I was not prepared for the excellence of the writing, nor for how very practical the book is. Joining her own considerable insights as a sensitive person with those of the scores of young people who have "experienced" her class, Yvonne has put together a readable, practical, and helpful book on nurturing a marriage.

If the test of a book on nurturing a marriage is how helpful it is to a young couple who would study it and discuss it together, then this book should be a best seller. The author covers all the essentials—but not so much in broad general ideas as in the very specific "for instances" in which they are dealt with in a marriage. Rather than giving a sociological treatise, she captures the essence of an idea in a phrase from a wife or a response from a husband. While the book reflects a solid knowledge of some of the best writing on the family, it is so much more than a gathering together of ideas. There is the sharing of fresh insight in understandable ways.

The style of the book is simple and direct. It is practical and readable. The questions at the close of each chapter could easily serve as a study guide for a couple or a class of couples.

The book reflects the insights of a woman who was watching her marriage a long time before beginning to help young couples to take a serious look at theirs. The book is a must for those who want to strengthen their marriage and those who want to help others with their marriages.

KENNETH L. CHAFIN

INTRODUCTION

I met my nephew John Robert when he got off the bus at the bus station. As we drove home, he explained that he had left home at eight o'clock that morning and that his dad had put him on the bus at twelve o'clock noon. I asked what he had done during those four hours, and he said he had sat in a court room and watched his father and other lawyers arguing a divorce case.

"One thing's for sure, I'm not ever gonna get divorced!" he said.

"Why?"

"Because it's so much trouble."

What John Robert didn't know, at age ten, was that staying married is a lot of trouble too. And much of that trouble surfaces during the first months of marriage.

Knowing this, the education staff of our church felt the need for a class for newlyweds. So five years ago, I moved from a median adult department, where I was leading a group in Family and Marriage, to our youngest adult section. There, I became a student! I learned what it's like to begin a marriage in the nuclear age. I was surprised to find out that the big problems are how to arrange visits with in-laws at Christmas, how to divide up home duties,

13

what to do about the weeping wife, and how to get rid of the husband's troublesome boy friends. I learned more. I learned that today's young marrieds do not enter into wedlock blindly. Most of them have long engagements, discuss feelings and dreams with each other, take Love and Marriage classes in college, and join enrichment groups after they marry. But even this conditioning does not prepare them wholly for the shocks and adjustments of learning to live together.

Our sessions are for six-month periods and are limited to an enrollment of twelve couples. Gene Vickrey, our Minister of Pastoral Care, suggested that the format be structured in three flexible divisions: acceptance, commitment and communication. All marriage problems, he said, will fall into one or more of these categories. (And all good marriages will be strong in these areas.) I have found this to be true.

I discovered that the members carried the class. One good question was all that was needed for a discussion that would easily go past our closing time. The value of the leader is to listen, keep eye-to-eye contact and pick up on statements or questions that can be used to emphasize, clarify, and entice. The prime caution is to be sure everyone is comfortable, that his/her comments and inquiries are given validity, and that *no one ever* is embarrassed. Humor is a must.

To be available outside class periods is another responsibility of the leader. Much of the conversation recorded in these chapters was recalled from private talks. Other jewels of information came from parties and meals in our homes, where husbands and wives shared their problems and their experiences.

I explained to my current group that when I quoted them in this book, I would not use their real names. They were quick to suggest that if they should say anything "profound," they'd like to be acknowledged! It's all "profound," and I really should be listing the names of 112 couples as our authors.

(I have used pseudonyms for class members, but real names for friends and relatives.)

Through the doors of those class rooms have come young couples overflowing with charm, mental and spiritual depth and incredible empathy. I am beguiled by them.

> Four things which I do not understand:
> The way of an eagle in the air,
> The way of a serpent on a rock,
> The way of a ship on the seas,
> And the way love grows between a man and a woman.
>
> *Agur, The Book of Proverbs*

1

INDIVIDUAL IDENTITIES

I felt it was necessary to explain to the group that Lisa and Allen were married to each other, in spite of the fact that they had different last names.

"Lisa just chose to keep her maiden name," I said.

Lisa said, "And Allen didn't want to change *his*."

Individual identities are important in marriage, but we achieve them in ways other than by having different names.

In many wedding ceremonies, the unity candle is used. This is an unlighted candle, representing the new relationship, which is placed between two single lighted candles representing the bride and groom. The new husband and wife simultaneously light the center candle with their individual candles as a symbol of unity. Kenneth Chafin says he always suggests to the couple that they not blow out their personal candles, as is often done, because even though they "now are one," they still are separate persons.

Handling dual careers

When we speak of individual identities, our thoughts seldom go beyond the work force. In careers, it is a simple matter to separate him from her, to compare talents, interests, problems, events of the day. Yet the difficulties that arise because of dual professions are results more of emotion than activity.

Camille Cates is a professional in urban management in Dallas. In discussing her course on the two-career family, she said, "It would be disastrous if anyone interpreted it as 'Step right up, folks, and buy your two-career marriage'; that's a sure way to mess things up."

We were discussing her statement in our class when Bill said he senses a certain unfairness in current trends. "The whole thing depends on your background, how you were raised. My dad was responsible for the family; he made the living. My mom stayed home. So there's no way I could step out of character and say to Diane, 'I think I'll quit working now and let you be the breadwinner.' She has a choice, but I don't."

What Alice said reverses the unfairness. "How about the wife whose career has really taken off, whose salary is greater, who finds it necessary to move to another town or work longer hours in order to enhance her career? We accept this if it's the husband, but we consider it radical if it's the wife."

We met Cathy and Howie at a reception for new teachers. They had just moved to the city. Howie had given up his job with an architecture firm when Cathy was hired as a member of the college faculty. He felt that he could find similar employment in his field, while jobs like Cathy's "are few and far between." Both were basking in their new situation.

The solution for Kay and Larry is more routine. Kay has been an English teacher in three different cities while Larry pursued his law career.

For most of the wives in our sessions, careers are temporary. They plan to quit at some point, at least for a few years, and raise a family. For them, the husband's job takes precedence.

Having children

When I quit working to have our first child, our income was cut in half and we had the added expenses of a new baby and our first car. For today's young couples, such a change is more traumatic. It is difficult to pay the mortgage and make the car payments without the second salary. To adjust to less money requires planning ahead, cutting back, and often help from parents. But it *can* be done—with practical discussions and frugal art.

Having children means an adjustment in more than family finances; children change our life styles. Many of the students in our classes feared the loss of identity with the onset of parenthood. This was particularly true of wives. They were afraid that when they were unable to pursue their careers on a full-time basis, their talents would go unrecognized and they would lose pace with the world.

For these and other reasons, some couples have chosen not to have children. Hopefully, this was a before-marriage agreement. Even so, we often detect a certain evasiveness about the reasons for remaining childless—such as blaming it on world conditions when the truth is "I don't want my life to change that much."

Many couples remain childless not because they planned to be, but because of prolonged postponement. They really anticipated having a baby or two someday when conditions were right. But in some cases, conditions were never right. In others, the years flew by and they felt they were too old to begin a family.

Turmoil abounds when a husband and wife are in disagreement about having children. This is a time for professional help.

Lance Morrow writes in *Time* that the United States appears to be growing up on the subject of children. "Today, many new parents start with the lowest expectations about having children—everyone has told them how sick the family is—and then awake in astonished delight to find that the experience is (or can be) wonderful."[1]

John Drakeford dedicated his book *The Home: Laboratory of Life*

> To my two sons . . .
> Who have put gray hairs in my head,
> Bills in my pocket,
> Illustrations in my sermons,
> Happiness in my home
> and Pride in my heart.[2]

Roles and duties

As Bill said, we are products of our environment. Even though a husband and wife leave the house in the morning and go their competent ways, the return home often finds them insecure about their roles. Who cooks dinner? Who pays the bills? Who cleans the bathroom?

Bonnie is great with cars. She is the family mechanic. Friends say they often find Bonnie under the hood of the automobile and Eric in the house running the vacuum or doing the dishes. Eric isn't at all bothered by this. He is grateful for an expert on the premises and definitely prefers working inside. "My psyche isn't damaged in the least."

Vicki's parents reversed traditional roles a generation ago. "Mother detested shopping. So Daddy did it all: groceries, clothes for my sister and me, Christmas presents, everything. He always cooked Sunday dinner. Even made my birthday cake one year! Mom paid the bills and worked in the yard and took care of most of the repair jobs around the house. They had a good marriage."

Allocation of home duties should be determined by

time and interest. If the husband arrives home from work before the wife does, he can start dinner. If she leaves the house later in the mornings, she can clean the kitchen and make the bed. Strict work assignments are often dangerous; they cause controversy and burdens of guilt when jobs are neglected. Flexibility is a major ingredient of working together.

Among newlyweds there are a few full-time housewives. Obviously, in these homes, the distribution of chores is different. Schedules are not as tight. However, it behooves any husband or wife to learn to handle the needs of the moment. There will be times of illness or separation that will require the knowledge of these skills. Besides, being helpful about the house—or the office or the yard—is a loving gesture.

Decisions

We are what we are largely by the decisions we make. And marriage is an endless round of decisions. Girls, more than boys, grow up struggling with choices. They carry into marriage their "I can'ts" and "what ifs." Making a decision is a lonely ordeal, but in marriage we expect help. How does one help a spouse make a decision? Charlie helped us answer that question.

Janet had trouble making up her mind on what to wear to work, whether or not to cut her hair, how to answer a letter. Then came the offer of a new job. Charlie listened to her sufferings until he knew he had to do something. He pooled his mental resources and recall. What had his parents done in such situations? What would the supervisors at the office say? He even thought back to a class he had in college on human behavior. He tried to understand Janet's dilemma. The one thing he knew was that he couldn't make the decision *for* her.

So on "the night of the great discourse," they talked.

They talked about her friends and co-workers at both places, the salaries and benefits, locations, transportation, hours, working conditions, chances for advancement, the challenges and enjoyment of the jobs, the mechanics and stresses of making a change. They listed priorities, considered their future plans. Finally Charlie assured her that once the decision was made, he would never bring up the subject again and that he certainly would not criticize her choice.

This gave Janet the security she needed. It also gave her a formula she continues to use. "And I've noticed that since I quit wasting so much time making decisions, I have more time for other things. Really. And I'm not constantly uptight."

The process is not always resolved so easily. And some couples are not involved in each other's mental battles. This may or may not be good. There are people who think silently and come up with conclusions. Fred was like this. Elizabeth had great faith in his decisions, but she was poised for shock. He would tell her of weekend plans he had made. Twice he contracted for a new apartment without consulting her. He bought a new suit that she didn't like. She had visions of his walking in some day and announcing that they were moving to Alaska or he had decided to become a deep sea diver. But the only time Elizabeth mentioned her frustrations to Fred was during the aftermath of his actions. He couldn't understand why she wanted to share in these drudgeries. He had not considered the anxiety of living with uncertainty.

Personal space and time

John found a note on the kitchen table when he came home late one night. It read: "Dearest John. Thank you for my evening at home. I'm glad you went to the ball game and that you didn't insist I go with you. It was fun being alone for a few hours, doing my own thing, even going to bed early. I'll return the favor some time soon. I love you. Pam."

In some marriages, the husband or wife travels from time to time or one has night classes or meetings. So finding time alone is not a problem. But for others, like John and Pam, there is a real need for personal space and time. John looked forward to his evening at home. Pam arranged for dinner and shopping with a friend. John came home with a new sports magazine and a pepperoni pizza, put his favorite records on the stereo and had "my kind of evening."

Kahlil Gibran wrote, "Let there be spaces in your togetherness." He explained that the oak tree and the cypress "do not grow in each other's shadow."[3] The same is true of people.

On the other hand, one can feel alone with a spouse sitting in the next chair. Evenings are made for sharing. During the early part of their marriage, Rhonda gave Sam a nightly quiz on the day's events, how he felt, what tomorrow would bring. After a couple of months of this, Sam decided he'd do away with the inquisition by giving a brief report as soon as he arrived home every day. His game turned out to be pure wisdom. Rhonda developed a keen insight into his work, his ideas, his problems, even the people in his office. Sam appreciated the periodic advice and comfort, and Rhonda felt a part of Sam's world. Sharing is affirming—an essential for growth in a person or in a marriage.

Marcie liked to sew, but she had done very little of it since she married. Dan didn't like the clutter. He blamed late meals and unfinished laundry on her sewing. He never complimented her on anything she made. So months ago Marcie closed up her sewing machine. Still she finds it depressing to spend money on clothes that she could make better and cheaper.

Talents should blossom in marriage. One has right at his elbow someone to encourage, critique, and assist. Both partners benefit. Sam could have had a happier, more grateful wife, even one who helped stretch the family dollar. Whether it's sewing or cooking or planting a garden, the very fact of the partnership requires support.

Differences—biological and acquired

Everyone is a product of the family in which he was raised. This means clashes in marriage. It makes essential an in-depth study of the feelings, fears, dreams, and reasonings of your spouse.

Doctors James Bossard and Eleanor Bell, in *The Girl That You Marry*, list two kinds of differences between husbands and wives: the biological and the acquired. The biological is obvious; the acquired refers to *learned* habits and ideas from our families, like being or not being affectionate, giving vent to emotions or holding them in.[4] Dr. Paul Tournier has written an entire book entitled *To Understand Each Other*.

For one couple, their biggest problem was that she felt bound by female requirements. Her husband considered it her duty to buy the groceries, to make the morning coffee, even to limit the places where she could be seen in slacks and jeans. At the same time, he considered himself the decision-maker, the social spokesman, the family provider. Her ideas were seldom heard. No job was thought to be beyond her call of duty. She was shriveling and the marriage was sagging.

In this case, the husband was able to continue in the philosophies of his environment, but the wife's identity was dwarfed. Marriage should be a pooling of characteristics with which we enhance each other. Again, discussion is needed.

Insurance for the future

Developing good individual identities is insurance for the future. Survival of the marriage depends on it. Survival of the person depends on it. Human resources will be needed to handle the crises of middle age, the empty nest, retirement, death of a spouse, illness, the many perils of parenthood. Such qualities also breed friendships, which are essentials of the good life.

We were talking about love one morning, what it really means, how we recognize it, how it grows after marriage. Lynn said, "I think the first time I really loved Greg—I mean *really* loved him—was on our first anniversary. He said to me, 'I think you should go visit your folks. I've had you for a whole year now. I can imagine how much they miss you.' The real Greg surfaced and I was consumed with love for him!"

Such empathy makes helping each other instinctive. And it is in helping each other that we develop our potential as loving, self-confident, valuable human beings.

DISCUSSION STARTERS

1. What do we mean by *identity?*

2. How is our sense of identity affected by childhood influences?

3. Is it fair for a wife to give up a good job in order for her husband to take a job in another city? How do we determine whose job is more important?

4. Is it an advantage or a disadvantage that these days we can decide whether or not we will have children?

5. On chalkboard make a list of responsibilities (purchase car, borrow money, accept invitations, choose friends, determine memberships, etc.). Should these always be *shared* responsibilities? If not, how does a couple decide who will be in charge?

6. From the situation with Janet and Charlie, construct a formula for decision-making.

7. What characteristics did Greg reveal when he suggested to Lynn that she visit her family?

8. If you were not married, what would you like best about being single?

9. If you had twenty-four hours to spend by yourself, without your spouse, what would you do? Give a

running schedule from waking up in the morning until going to bed at night. (This question gives the responder an opportunity to bask in thoughts of favorite pastimes and gives his or her spouse a look into his/her wishes.)

2

EMOTIONAL AND PERSONALITY DIFFERENCES

Dr. James Dobson writes, "Males and females differ biochemically, anatomically, and emotionally. In truth they are unique in every cell of their bodies."[1]

Nancy and Kirk agree. For sure. "If someone had told me," said Nancy, "that I would spend half my time crying after I was married, I would have said, 'No way.'" She was flabbergasted at her reservoir of tears. During the first few weeks of marriage, she cried in the kitchen, in the bedroom, in the bathroom, the car, everywhere. Kirk ran the gamut of shock to laughter. He was afraid to talk and not talk, to touch her, to keep hands off. Nancy couldn't explain. She was a failure in the kitchen. She fluctuated between wanting to make love and not wanting to, without reason. She would think of something she forgot to buy at the market and cry. She'd weep over a mound of laundry. Once Kirk suggested she call and talk to her parents and she couldn't see through her tears to dial the number. Menstrual periods were almost as hard on him as they were on her.

Nancy only knows that at these times, the tears came. They just came. "I cried more in one month than I'd cried in my entire twenty-three years." She and Kirk are convinced men and women are different.

This is not a rare scene. Many a husband has felt devastated by the complexity of the girl he married. At the same time, wives find it difficult to adjust to the little boy in their husbands. How much of this is the result of our society in a continuous debate. Little boys don't cry; girls don't cuss. Boys play football; girls take ballet. Yet we do know that numerous ailments can be triggered in females because of hormonal imbalance. We also know that, regardless of the origin of differences, couples take into marriage conflicting surprises. It takes patience to create stability.

Expressing feelings

In our class surveys of "My major weakness as a husband," a leading answer is the inability to express feelings. The fellows say they are embarrassed and sometimes even angry at being expected to tell all. Yet they don't like feeling this way. One husband said that even if he could be at ease, he wouldn't know *how* to say what he felt.

This was not a problem of the wives. Rather, they expressed a need to practice restraint in vocalizing feelings. We agreed that there is a need for a meeting of the minds, a climate for comfortable sharing.

Dr. Paul Tournier espouses the idea that *man* has a theoretical mind while *woman* has a "person-centered" mind. He explains that women think in terms of people; men expound theories. Women think in detail; men find details unimportant.

Mike said he could testify to this. When he goes out of town on business, for example, Susan wants to know who is going with him, what that person's wife will do while they're gone, who the people are that they'll be working with. When he discusses a project or conference at the office, she'll interrupt with, "Wasn't that embarrassing for him?" or, "Why do you think he felt that way?" To Mike, the reasons and the people are not pertinent.

Still, these differences help husbands and wives to complement each other. There is something leveling about the way opposites get together: the extrovert and introvert, the sentimentalist and realist, the artist and the intellectual.

Opposites attract

Fran is an artist. In every sense of the word. She paints in water colors and oils. She plays the piano. She sees dimension in a sunset and beauty in a piece of driftwood. And she is married to Ed, a space scientist, who sees sun as a source of energy and wood as building material. To him imagination is for use only as an estimate. Still, he and Fran are beautiful together. He admires her finished products, and she is awed at his abilities. Their priorities and goals are the same, and they have an abundance of friends.

Helen and Phil, on the other hand, are not as much alike socially as Fran and Ed are. Phil is the friend-maker. He has an inexhaustible supply of jokes; he has a knack for making everyone in the room feel at ease. Including Helen. She depends on him. She is quiet and discerning. But she laughs at Phil's banter; she revels in his charm.

Several sentimentalist-realist combinations come to mind, but Vivian and Charlie are the classic example. Vivian is a scrapbook maker, a saver of letters and ribbons, a reader of verse and prose, a teacher of English and history. Charlie is a petroleum engineer, an advocate of efficiency, a businessman, a protective husband and father. They are not newlyweds. Vivian and Charlie have been married almost thirty years and have raised four fantastic children. Painful give-and-take has been a way of life, a game of mutual concession and retreat.

Early in their marriage, when possessions were stored in relatives' garages and attics, Vivian was arranging to move to their apartment a box of nostalgic treasures. Charlie rebelled. He stood in the center of the room and, in an uncharacteristic gesture, raised his hand and proclaimed, "Tomorrow is gone forever and you can't bring it back!" His botched declaration has become a family slogan. And Charlie has learned to live with scrapbooks and frivolity.

Products of influences

Other emotional types are products of many influences: family, neighborhood, peers, school, even communications media. There is no self-made man. Or woman. Which is not to say we should go through our adult lives blaming our parents and circumstances for what we are. Rather, we need to lay strong hold on our positive qualities and downgrade our negatives. Above all, young marrieds must recognize the sources of their spouses' makeup and roll with the punches.

When our son Richard was a toddler, he tracked me down in the bedroom, took my hand, led me to the kitchen, positioned me in front of the sink and said, "Stay there." The world is filled with Richards who grow up and get married and find security in a woman in the kitchen. Likewise, there are wives for whom being a homemaker is a fulfilled dream—and others for whom it is most unfulfilling.

In *Passages*, Gail Sheehy says "First-born daughters are often brought up with privileges and expectations no different from a son's. (They are taught by fathers—and

mothers—to emphasize abilities and carry family responsibilities)."[2]

You may be married to a first daughter or a second or
third one. Each is a reflection of her parents and grandparents and sets the table and folds the socks as she was
taught. To change the basic pattern, more is needed than
a constant harangue from one's spouse of "that is stupid"
or "you must be kidding."

After all, you too are a chip off the block, whether it's
by imitation or rebellion. By "dos" and "don'ts" you've
developed habits and temperaments that make you you.

Raymond said, "Getting married and having your own
home really changes you. Here you are, trying to retain
your single life style, to be your own man, and little by
little it gets displaced by more mature thinking."

"My father died when I was very young," said Gwen,
"so my influences were all female: my mother, grandmother, aunts. Being concerned about this, Mom would,
from time to time, try to invade my world with a father-
figure. First, it was an uncle. Then she arranged for a
neighbor to share his time with his daughter with me
also. I even took a summer vacation trip with them. But I
was always more comfortable with the women. I still am.
My strongest male influence was a tenth-grade biology
teacher who was also my basketball coach. But I wouldn't
say he taught me a great deal about men."

Gwen may be unaware of what she did learn from her
teacher. All relationships color our lives and contribute to
the whole. We *must* accept these differences.

Dealing with fears

When it comes to emotions, right up there at the top are
fears. Everyone has them. And, in marriage especially,
they need to be expressed. By wives *and* husbands. This
was done in our classes, and the results are beneficial to

list here. The number one fear was rejection. The other nine, in order of importance, were:

2. Loneliness.
3. Poor health.
4. Death.
5. Old age.
6. Child-rearing.
7. Finances, loss of income.
8. Natural disasters.
9. Lack of friendships.
10. In-laws.

Husbands	*Wives*
1. Poor health.	1. Rejection.
2. Old age.	2. Loneliness.
3. Rejection.	3. Death.
4. Loss of income.	4. Old age.
5. Death.	5. Child-rearing.
6. Child-rearing.	6. Lack of friendships.
7. Loneliness.	7. Poor health.
8. Lack of friendships.	8. Natural disasters
9. In-laws.	9. Loss of income.
10. Natural disasters.	10. In-laws.

The male-female breakdown in this list was enlightening. Wives feared rejection, loneliness, death (more of loved ones than self) and natural disasters. Husbands were more concerned with poor health, old age, and loss of income. What we see here is the strong drive in man to be the competent provider, to be uninterrupted in his quest for success. The wives, to a large degree, were troubled about relationships. Where the husband was concerned with providing, the wife was concerned with protecting and being protected.

Insecurity often surfaced as jealousy. Leah expressed

this feeling when she said, "When I see Barney with some other girl, I know it doesn't mean a thing, but something in me cringes." Maxine said she tried not to think about all the girls Harvey worked with every day, because when she did, she got "this knot in my stomach." Rosa could understand their feelings even though she didn't consider jealousy a problem. She didn't like staying alone at night. "I have to keep reminding myself," she said, "that this isn't permanent, that Derk really is coming home eventually."

Franklin voiced the fears of many husbands when he admitted that the reason buying a house was such a monumental decision for him was the fear of financial reverses. "If I should lose my job, even for a few months, or if I had to spend time recuperating from an illness, we'd lose the house, for sure."

If you are afraid of storms, say so. Julie did. And her astute husband Tom was alert to opportunities to help her. They walked in the rain, met a storm coming in from the coast, and shared and discussed the sounds of thunder.

Sid's fear of missing out on friendships caused him to go overboard on entertaining and being with people. Jennifer was surprised to learn fear was involved; she thought he was "just extremely outgoing."

For the first year of her marriage, Wendy pretended to like horses, country music and camp-outs—because that was what Paul liked. Not until she confessed were she and Paul able to work out a compromise.

Whether it's a fear, a strong like or dislike, anger, jealousy, revenge, sympathy, generosity—whatever—it should be shared. Bottled-up feelings are cancerous to marriage.

One reason women live longer than men, we are told, is because they can express emotion in a way that is socially acceptable; they can "fall apart" without being disgraced.

We are a humanity of unlikes. First, because God made us male and female; then, because we have lived in the midst of people and situations that have fashioned us. It is the purpose of marriage not to refashion but to embellish.

DISCUSSION STARTERS

1. When was the first time after marriage that you (your wife or husband) cried? Why? What was your wife's (your husband's) reaction?

2. On unsigned cards or pieces of paper, list what you consider your major weakness as a husband or wife. Divide in male and female categories and discuss.

3. Do you agree with Dr. Tournier's theory that men and women *think* differently? Why? Give an example to support your opinion.

4. What do you consider the greatest emotional difference between the male and the female?

5. Do you know opposites who are married to each other? If the marriage is working well, why? If not, why?

6. What are the strong influences on our lives today? Do you think the situation is different from a generation ago? A century ago?

7. What are you most afraid of? Is this a fear from childhood? If not, how do you account for it? What can be done about it?

8. What makes you angry? Why?

9. Use a role-playing situation in which the husband announces to the wife that he will be flying out-of-town on business next week and she and other wives have been invited to go along. After several futile excuses, the wife admits that she is afraid of planes. The husband examines the source of her fear and presents ideas for helping her.

10. Which is stronger: heredity or environment?

3

INTIMACY

The dictionary defines "intimacy" as "a close personal relationship." The second meaning is "sexual intercourse." To reverse the two puts marriage on a collision course. Counselors agree that the close personal relationship is the essential; sex is a part of that relationship. Passion enhances a union, gives it life, satisfies longings, but it is not a substantial hook on which to hang a marriage.

Ray Short, University of Wisconsin sociologist, says his studies show that marriages based on sex attraction last three to five years. "The average American couple," he says, "spends less than half an hour a week in sexual intercourse. If you marry mainly for sex, tell me, what in heaven's name will you do the rest of the time?"[1]

Let's look at that "rest of the time"—the components of intimacy.

What do you mean when you say to your spouse, "I love you?" Our group was responding to this question:

"I mean that I appreciate you."
"I'm glad I married you."
"I want you to be happy."
"Having you makes it all worthwhile."

"You're funny."

"I want to be close to you."

"Sometimes," said Ted, "I say 'I love you' as an invitation, sort of."

Much of what marrieds do is an invitation for affection. Signs of love nourish the spirit as food nourishes the body. Affection is a necessity.

The importance of saying "I love you"

For Jane, the honeymoon was a nightmare. "One would have thought I was a sex maniac," she said. "The only time I got attention from Roger was in bed. So I could have *lived* there. I needed affection; I wanted Roger to tell me he loved me. But he didn't. Ever. I'd go for two or three days, then I'd blow my top. Roger really couldn't understand this. He said I should know he loved me, that he loved his family, but he didn't have to go around telling them so. 'But I'm not your family and you *do* have to tell *me* so,' I screamed. So he began working at it. It was very difficult for him because it was something he had never done. There was no show of affection in his home—absolutely none. I watched him suffer. But he learned to touch and to say 'I love you.' It's marvelous."

Wives, more than husbands, want love verbalized. Husbands accept a clean house or a special meal as an expression of love. For both, holding hands, sitting side by side, the hug, the kiss, the pat, a wink from across the room, even a familiar tilt of the head or shrug of the shoulders can bring skyrockets to the soul. One therapist says every married person should learn to give massages, that it speaks volumes of love as well as being beneficial physically.

(Incidentally, tickling is not affection. It more often is described as sadism.)

There is nothing wrong with saying what you like.

More husbands and wives would express love the way their mates want it, if they only knew what those mates prefer.

Whatever your mode of affection, don't lose it. Practice it, cherish it, even make a habit of it. Katy was very moved by the fact that her father-in-law, after thirty years of marriage, still kisses his wife as he seats her at the dinner table.

It was suggested in our group that everyone should make a conscious effort to say "I love you" at least three times a day. Millie took the suggestion seriously. Several weeks later, she reported that she had "really worked hard at that." "Yes," said Donald, "sometimes she goes overboard to be sure she has covered all three; sometimes she doesn't get that third one in until I've been asleep for an hour!"

Saying it with loving behavior

Intimacy requires more than whispers of love and romantic gestures. It requires action. We made a list for you of loving behavior ideas, tried and true ones:

Putting a note in the lunchbox,
> or cookbook,
> or suitcase,
> or pocket,
> or on the pillow
> or mirror.
> (Dora even left one in the shower stall. And Gloria leaves one on the kitchen table for those days when Al arrives home before she does.)

Peforming an unpleasant task without being asked. (Cleaning the bathroom and taking out the garbage seem to be winners.)
Bringing home an un-birthday present.
Reading aloud.

Giving sex high priority by devoting an evening to it, as you would a dinner party.

Writing a letter to the in-laws. (Bruce called Carol's father and mother when he and Carol had their first anniversary to say thanks for their daughter.)

Putting flowers or candles on the dinner table. Or breakfast table.

Using statements with "I thought about you today when—" or questions like "Do you remember the time—?"

And how about this one? Scott "goes around whistling or humming a tune—a new one every day nearly—and asking, 'Remember that?' or, 'What does this remind you of?'"

The "I dos" at a wedding ceremony do not guarantee anything. There is nothing automatic or natural about a happy marriage; it requires constant vigilance. Meaning hard work.

Sorting out your expectations

Counselors agree that a major reason for divorce among young people is that they go into marriage with unrealistic expectations. This is especially true of sexual experiences. The couple keeps hoping these problems will resolve themselves, when actually they need to be talked out. In some cases, a visit to the family doctor is advisable.

Dr. Joyce Brothers writes, "People want more from marriage and from love than older generations ever demanded or expected. . . . Many marriages fail because the two persons involved have never been able to get around their notions of the 'ideal' mate long enough to see what is really there. When the image is shattered, they may be disappointed and disillusioned."[2]

Dr. Jessie Potter, director of the National Institute for Human Relationship, agrees. "This is the first time in the history of the world that people have asked for intimacy,

communication, sensuality and quality sex in their marriages."[3]

A study by the Esalen Institute concludes: "Marriage is
now burdened with the expectations that husbands and
wives should enjoy intellectual companionship, intimate,
warm moments, shared values, deep romantic love and
great sexual pleasures. Couples expect more, and their
new expectations often clash with traditional values. The
result is that many people feel they're missing out."

If these are *your* expectations, you'll have to *make* them
happen. And remember, you can't have everything—in
marriage or in any other part of life. As one husband of
many years said, "Don't worry about what you may be
missing; just be grateful for what you have."

Being friends

John and Abigail Adams wrote many letters to each
other, all beginning with "My Lover, My Friend." And so
it should be. Your husband or wife, hopefully, is your
best friend. So what do you do with a best friend? Talk?
Laugh? Play tennis? Share news? Eat lunch? What do you
do *for* a best friend? Buy gifts? Plan parties? Give moral
support?

Often Emily found herself shopping or at home watching TV while Matt went to ball games. Especially on
Saturdays. Finally she retaliated. She read a book called *A
Wife's Football Handbook* and became a fan of not only
football, but other sports. Now she and Matt go together.
"It costs twice as much that way," said Matt, "so I go half
as often."

Such situations should be discussed. A wife with
Emily's problem could begin by admitting she's lonely or
jealous or resentful. Probably the husband would be
flattered. At least, he'd get the message. Hopefully, she
would add, "I want to be with you. I miss the fun. You

are the most important person in the world to me." Or whatever makes him flip out. Feelings are to be shared. Particularly in marriage.

The importance of touching

Dr. Potter talks of our "touch-deprived" society. "If a Martian came here," she says, "he would frequently hear talk about being 'in touch' and about people who are 'touchy,' 'soft touches,' 'easy touches,' and 'very touching.' That little stranger would think touch is really important down here. But he would almost never see physical touching and would have a hard time figuring out what the word meant."

If people touched more throughout their lives, she says, "there would be less mediocre sex and more people might find marriage a warm, nurturing place to be."

In his book *Making Contact*, Dr. Arthur Wassmer writes, "The eventual deterioration of *contact* in marriage is the single most common marital problem, occurring more often than incidences of adultery, physical brutality, financial mismanagement and sexual incompatibility combined."[4] That is powerful!

Love should be a form of communication, he says, a very special form. What couples should be saying to each other is, "I am interested in who you are. I want to hear about your thoughts and feelings. I want to experience your body. I want to share in your happenings." And—get this—the most important message is "and I want you to feel the same way about me."

Glynn explained to the counselor that things were better sexually for him and Beverly after he "began to seek for fulfillment for her rather than for myself." And this came about only after they learned to discuss their problems. Liz Smith, in *The Mother Book*, tells of a Victorian woman who endured her wedding night by gritting her teeth and "thinking of England."[5] Beverly's experience was not quite like this, but she *had* gone into marriage, she said, thinking of the husband as the decision-maker in sex activities and the wife as the follower. But she didn't like this arrangement and also found it awkward to talk about it. She felt trapped. This was when she took it upon herself to visit a therapist.

"So," she said, "tell people not to assign duties and responsibilities. Sometimes when I feel turned on, Glynn doesn't. And vice versa. We both understand this now and neither of us feels mistreated."

"And set up your own patterns," said Sue. "I think this is what bothered me so much when I first got married. I had a major in family relations and I'd read all the books on marriage. Brian and I did not conform to the 33 percent of the particular poll that was being taken, and I thought something was wrong. Then I finally read somewhere that whatever you establish as your pattern, one that you're comfortable with, that's fine."

To expect the bedroom scene to be perfect from the beginning is unrealistic. A group of couples, married an average of ten years each, answered a questionnaire on how long it took to reach a mutually satisfactory adjustment in their sex lives. The results: from two weeks to nine years. The adjustment, in most cases, was directly related to the ability of the couples to communicate with each other.

Denise said, "Sometimes in the evening, when it's early and we're watching TV or reading or working, I see Will across the room and I'd like to go sit by him and snuggle up, but I don't, because I know we'd end up in the bedroom. Before we were married, we held hands and hugged and even kissed. I don't get that anymore; I just get sex."

For many couples, this is the beginning of the loss of affection. At an appropriate time, Denise would be wise to express her yearning to Will, explain her feeling of loss *and* her desire to show her love.

Four thousand American males were asked, "How do you feel about hugging and kissing without its leading to sexual intercourse?" Seventy one percent said they liked it. The results of the survey, presented in the book *Beyond the Male Myth,* showed that most of the men felt that such signs of affection usually "elicit strong positive feelings."[6] One man wrote, "Just after having a fight with my wife, or when I am feeling low and I need her companionship and love, I think hugging is great. It gives me a warm feeling."

Andy said, "I wouldn't ever want to lose the fun of holding hands and kissing. And being kissed."

Most husbands and wives find the endearments mutually enjoyable and, like Andy, wouldn't want to lose them. But the time to be alert to the danger of such loss is in the early months of marriage. Take a lesson from Millie; be sure to get that third "I love you" in.

Making love: fears, fantasies, and fun

Still, praise be, there is that difference, that uniqueness of male and female. True to her nature, the female is concerned with feelings and reasons and propriety. She is likely to be concerned about privacy, and she prefers a quiet house and a dark bedroom. She is a true advocate of "the night was made for love." She, according to Dr. James Dobson, is turned on more by the sense of touch than the sense of sight. "The physiological mechanism of sex is not triggered typically by what she sees; a woman is stimulated primarily by the sense of touch. Thus, we encounter the first source of disagreement in the bedroom; he wants her to appear unclothed in a lighted room, and she wants him to caress her in the dark."

Dr. Potter says man "has this scenario in his head that

makes it possible for him to turn himself on." "He is excited by a photograph of a nude woman or a scantily clad one walking down the street, even though," says Dr. Dobson, "he knows nothing about her personality or values or mental capabilities." A wife may flip over Robert Redford or her physics professor, but her involvement usually goes beyond the physical.

Then there are all those fears that keep us in check, such as the fear of pregnancy. (You and your doctor should be able to care for this one.) Some people take into marriage unhealthy attitudes about sex. Wives have visions of being rejected because they're not beautiful or they're not performing satisfactorily. Husbands have been led to believe that macho depends upon perfection in love-making. Often inhibitions need to be shaken off in order for sex to be its best. Fatigue, illness, worry all take their toll.

Being sensitive to any of these problems is an imperative for the loving husband or wife.

Marriage should be spiced with love-making that is more than being close and sharing the same bed. It should be a union of mischievousness, laughter, passion, dried tears, and shared expectations.

Jack Smith, in *Spend All Your Kisses, Mr. Smith*, writes: "Why keep a kiss, a gesture, a word that might give a moment's pleasure or reassurance to someone else? Money you can't take with you. Kisses you can't leave behind. So spend all your kisses."[7]

DISCUSSION STARTERS

1. Did you ever wish to be a member of the opposite sex? When? Why?

2. What do you mean when you say, "I Love you"?

3. List ways you would like your mate to show affection. (Use un-signed cards for your answers.)

4. Name something your spouse has done to show his/her love—notes, doing chores, etc.

5. Take a survey of your group (secret ballot) and discuss results: "What do you feel are the major anxieties newlyweds have about sex relationships?"

6. List the probable causes of these anxieties.

7. Do you think Denise's problem is a common one for new wives?

8. Should acts of affection become habits? Why? Why not?

4

LIKING YOURSELF

To be married to a person with a poor self-image is horrendous. Marriage does not *produce* this low self-esteem, but it *can* reinforce it. Or dispel it. As a rule, a low conception of one's self begins in childhood, often from infancy.

Brad and Abby were the typical case of the popular, confident husband and the meek, insecure wife. "I worshiped him from afar," said Abby. "He was the BMOC at college, then was the graduate assistant in my economics class. I don't know why he married *me*; I was a nothing." Abby was raised by a widowed mother who felt the world had dealt her a bitter blow. Being her mother's major responsibility, Abby considered herself a big part of the problem. Her mother never had the time or inclination to give Abby the emotional support she needed. So, in spite of a good academic record and numerous friendships in college, Abby saw nothing in herself to attract a person like Brad. But then Brad explained to her that he would not have such self-assurance if it had not been for his supportive family. Now Abby is thriving on love and admiration from Brad *and* from her in-laws.

Counselors tell us that low self-esteem is a leading cause of problems they see in their clients, problems such as doubts and depression. These patients dislike what they see in their mirrors. A common word used in describing themselves is "stupid." They are sure the world would be just as good without them. To burden a marriage with these feelings is dangerous business.

But what if you are married to someone like this? What if *you* are the self-belittler?

Remember that being human means *we need to be needed*.

Brad made it clear to Abby that he needed her. His complexity needed her simplicity. His outrage needed her calm. Her logic compensated for his irrationality. "She is my map-reader, my navigator, my inspiration. And she makes me laugh."

Marriage means freedom from embarrassment

Nothing is more crippling to the ego than feeling ashamed. If you have caused or allowed your spouse to be embarrassed, no amount of apology erases the stigma.

Marge remembers with affection friends of her parents who never allowed each other to be embarrassed. "I've watched him bail her out by changing the subject with such finesse that no one noticed. And if his joke or statement did not receive proper response, she would give it the necessary climax."

"I promised Stu I'd love him forever," said Sandy, "because of the way he rescued me one evening. I made an innocent reference that sounded for all the world as if it were intended for the couple sitting across from us. Stu intercepted with something like 'That happened to me once' and went on to get everyone caught up in *his* story."

"I guess the most embarrassed I ever was," said Wayne, "was the time I got a ticket for jay-walking. Midge was standing across the street waiting for me, watching the whole thing. Not that day or since has she mentioned it to me or to anyone else."

Keep on reassuring

Maybe it's the wife who insists on being told every hour on the hour that she is loved. Or it could be the husband who constantly needs the verbal pat on the back.

Remember Tevye in *Fiddler on the Roof*, asking Golde if she still loved *him*? She pointed out that she had been a faithful wife for many years, had kept house, cooked meals, mothered four daughters; wasn't that answer enough? But that wasn't the kind of reassurance Tevye was seeking; he wanted the "I love you" which means "you're special."

An announcement on the wedding day is not enough. Encouragement needs to be kept updated.

"When I complain," said Jill, "I feel like an idiot if Mark doesn't support me. Like if I explain an incident and he says I shouldn't have gotten involved or maybe I misunderstood or maybe they didn't mean it that way, well, I feel rotten. What I want him to do is really hear me out, then, somehow, make me feel better about it."

This is an imperative of marriage, that we have not only a shoulder to cry on but a balm for the spirits.

Know when the build-up is needed

Burt felt like a very unobservant husband when someone asked, "What's wrong with Wanda? Is she sick or is she just preoccupied?" He had been so busy and so tired and so full of his own problems that he had hardly looked at Wanda. She was aware of his hectic schedule, so she hadn't bothered him with her worries. This situation, prolonged, could have been perilous.

We see the signals if we are alert to them: questions, moody behavior, rare quietness, the bid for attention. Eileen recognized Gib's lows by the tapping of his feet

and the "far-away look in his eyes." When Tammy is
blue, she goes to bed early. Ross drives too fast. Alex flits
from one thing to another.

It's rough to feel sad alone.

Empathy means "I know how you feel"

Rachel read somewhere that there should be complete
honesty in marriage, that husband and wife should share
everything from their pasts. She asked Bart his opinion.
"Do you want me to tell you *everything* from my past?"
she asked. "Only the part that doesn't make you hurt,"
he said.

Encourage, but don't push

We were having dinner in our friends' very formal
dining room. And I was on my thirty-second diet of the
year. Vernon made it a point to help the hostess serve. He
passed the bread behind my back and gave me a mere
sliver of pie. I appreciated his quiet encouragement.

Janice was taking a night course in typing. She really
wanted to learn to type, but she hated the lessons;
actually she hated typing. Curt prodded her to be at
school every Tuesday and Thursday night; he even did
the kitchen chores, often took her out to eat, and always
took her to school and picked her up. But he bugged her
about practicing. If she decided to read or watch TV or
work on her needlepoint, he insisted her time should be
spent at the typewriter. "If it hadn't been for the tuition
money we'd spent," said Janice, "I would have quit—just
to spite him. He had no concern for my feelings; his only
interest was in my learning to type."

The kind of push we most often need in marriage is not
the hard drive; it's the gentle shove. Yet, on rare occasions, the firm prod may be needed.

"My father had this theory about food," said Marsha, "that if it's good, Mom knows it; if it's bad, she *needs* to know it. So he commented only on the *bad* food. I couldn't wait to tell him that at our house, it's different; if it's bad, Wes doesn't say anything, but if it's good, he tells me."

Help yourself to like yourself

But how? First of all, *speak up.* Let it be known that you want help. But don't let it be an excuse for slovenliness. Angie was having difficulty coping with the pupils in her fourth grade class. She came home from school every day and went to bed. To Earl's complaints about no dinner and a sloppy house, she had a pat answer: "I can't; I don't feel good." She foiled her chance for sympathy—and help—from Earl.

Chip hated himself for being overweight, but he liked to eat. When, finally, he involved wife, family, friends and co-workers in his weight loss program, he found the support he had been needing.

Dawn was constantly setting goals she didn't reach. She would leave one job unfinished to start another one. She would make big plans for the weekend and "look back on Sunday night at all my failures." Her reformation came about when she learned to limit her projects to one at a time, to make short-term plans, and to anticipate the unscheduled events that are part of every life, especially in marriage.

Cut out what Mark Short calls "Pity Parties." Quit feeling sorry for yourself. Count your blessings. Latch on to the affirmative. Look around you. Then—

Read. Observe. Become knowledgeable. Be a good conversationalist. Back in the sixteenth century, Leonardo da Vinci said, "Learning maketh the soul young; it decreaseth the bitterness of old age."

Accept responsibility for yourself. "The best years of your life," writes Dr. Albert Ellis, "are the ones in which you decide your problems are your own. You don't blame them on your mother, your environment, the ecology or the President. You realize that you control your own destiny."[1]

"In my last job," said Liz, "I sat at a desk next to a girl who really helped me. Every time I complained about something or someone, she'd say, 'Well, don't blame her', or, 'That's *your* fault.' One day I asked her, 'Is everything that happens to me my fault?' 'Sure,' she answered. Well, I think she was a bit too cocksure of herself, but she really got me to thinking."

Lydia said, "I used to blame my problems on the fact that I'm so short. I couldn't run fast, I couldn't reach the top shelf. I couldn't find the kind of clothes I liked. Then I came to grips one day with the fact that this is as tall as I'm going to be, that I can't waste my time cursing my size, that there *are* advantages in being short, and that most things in life do not require height. Mostly, I just grew up—though not far up!—and accepted the situation. I'm learning to find other things to blame for my problems."

Reach out to someone else. Get out of the house. Enlarge your horizon. Take a meal to a shut-in. Baby-sit for a friend. Visit someone in the hospital. Get to know your neighbors. Entertain a foreign student. Become a good listener.

Open your home. Give a party. Invite out-of-town friends for the weekend. Have another couple in for the evening. Offer your home for a neighborhood or political meeting or church group.

Spend quality time with your spouse. This doesn't mean you have to take in a movie or a ball game. When Valerie feels really bad about herself, she likes a "deep sharing time" with Wynn. "Really, I don't want to *share* so much as I want him to talk. I want to get involved in his world. I want to hear everything he will tell me. It helps to remind me that I'm not alone, that I have Wynn."

The media are so filled with messages about how charming and successful and happy we should be that it is easy for us to feel we're not making the grade. However, our lives must be lived out in the real world, not the tinsel one. Believe your wife when she tells you you're the greatest—and your husband when he says the smartest thing he ever did was to marry you.

In one of our sessions each person turned in an anonymous card on which was written "My strongest quality as a husband or wife is—." One husband wrote: "It is difficult for me to express any positive characteristics about myself. For various reasons, I have been convinced that to so speak of one's self is boastful, bragging from a position of self-centeredness. Probably this is my largest stumbling block."

He has taken the first step, that of recognizing his problem. Hopefully, his wife says "I love you" very, very often.

After all, we are "wonderfully made,"
"In God's image,"
"A little lower than the angels."

DISCUSSION STARTERS

1. As you were growing up, who complimented you most often?

2. Name an incident from your childhood that boosted your ego.

3. Can you recall a situation in which your assistance was invaluable to people involved?

4. In your opinion, what does a man most like to be complimented on? (One such survey had as the top six: good looks, physique, love-making, clothes, conversation, and job.) Compile answers.

5. What phrase does a wife like most to hear? Compile answers. (Such a survey listed "I love you," "You look nice," "You're beautiful," and "You have lost weight.")

6. Recall an embarrassing moment, in childhood or recently. What was the outcome? Why do you still remember it?

7. On unsigned cards, answer the question "How do you know when your spouse needs help with his or her feelings?" Collect the answers and have someone read them to the group.

8. How *do* you encourage without pushing?

9. Discuss areas of help to others that are available in your city.

10. Suggest ways for a couple to spend quality time together.

11. List some of your good feelings (such as wearing new hose, smelling gingerbread, hearing the national anthem, etc.).

12. On unsigned cards list "My husband's (wife's) strongest marriage quality is—" Put list on chalkboard. Ask each husband, each wife, "Which of these do you think your spouse submitted?" Conclude by asking, "How many of your mates chose the right entry?" (Do not identify authors; keep it private.)

5

IN-LAWS AND
FAMILY

Our friends' son was explaining why he had stopped
dating his latest girlfriend. "Well, you remember last
week at Grandma's when we were all standing around
the dining table, holding hands and singing the Doxol-
ogy? Well, I decided she just wouldn't fit in somehow."

Families do make a difference.

Our ideals, our habits, prejudices, likes and dislikes,
rights and wrongs, and, to some extent, even our personalities are the results of many generations of ancestors.

When we asked, "Which parent is your wife most
like?" Nick said, "She isn't like either parent; she's like
her grandmother."

"You really marry a family system," explained Mona.
"Whether you live across the country from your parents
or in the same town with them, you can't be separated
from the *real* emotional field of the family."

Tim added to this: "When we became engaged, I was
trying to explain to Doreen all the eccentricities of my
folks, and she said, 'Well, I'm not marrying your *family*.' I
told her, 'Oh yes, you *are!*'"

And so it is.

Home—*an extension of two families*

The new home established by newlyweds is an exten-
sion of the two homes from which they came. Ryan said,

"We had been married only a few weeks and were living in a small apartment when one day I started seeing things in our lives and in our place that I remembered from my own home. I always thought it would be different. I hoped it would be different."

On the other hand, Marilyn says she feels good about Lance because he is so much like her father. "We remind me of my parents more and more, and I like that."

I clipped from a Washington, D.C., newspaper a provocative article on the importance of brothers and sisters. Psychoanalyst Dr. Walter Toman believes that the prosperity of a couple's marriage (and other relationships) is largely predetermined by the partners' age and sex position within their families. For example, the marriages most likely to succeed, according to the report, are those made of: (1) the older brother of a sister *and* the younger sister of a brother; or, (2) the younger brother of a sister *and* the older sister of a brother.[1]

This theory of "complementary sibling roles" is widely accepted in the psychiatric profession because of the effect it has on marriages. The husband or wife goes into the new relationship experienced in relating closely to the opposite sex.

Many husbands are shocked at the crying sessions of their new wives. But a boy who grows up with a sister understands the tears. Wives are prepared for their husbands' preoccupation with sports because they had brothers.

And yet, many do not fit into this sibling role. What then? Dee said one of the most important lessons she learned was from her older sister. "She helped prepare me for marriage by telling me about men. And not about just my brother-in-law, but husbands of her friends, about their needs, their ups and downs, how to adjust, what to expect, etc."

Marian Martin, writing in *Home Life*, explains that she

came from a kissing family of three daughters, while her husband was from a nonkissing family of boys, and her husband considered all the affection "overdone and embarrassing."[2]

She goes on to point out that just as all-girl and all-boy families give different experiences to children, so do large families versus small ones. "The size of a family affects the grown person's feelings about noise, activity, and privacy. A large family will do more sharing of room and household furnishings by necessity, and will accept this sharing as a matter of course in later years."

We learn from cousins and from close friends. From parents and grandparents. From teachers and coaches. No one is self-made. Each is a composite of everyone and everything that has touched his life. Your husband is. Your wife is. And so are you.

On your own

This leaving father and mother is not easy. Some parents hold on more tightly than others. Some sons and daughters are more dependent than others. However, we are finding an abundance of good relationships with parents these days, particularly with mothers and mothers-in-law. Reuben Herring says the in-law problem usually is a mother-in-law problem. The home and family are extensions of the woman's world. "If the father-in-law still took his young son into partnership with him, then the problem might as often have to do with the meddling father-in-law."[3]

One mother said, "It isn't so much that we find it hard to give up our baby as it is that we want the marriage to work, we see their mistakes and we interfere when we shouldn't."

One hundred wives were asked the question, "What does your mother-in-law most often criticize you about?"

The results: (1) cooking, (2) housekeeping, (3) children, (4) weight and figure and (5) not calling or visiting. Possibly the most illuminating information was that most daughters-in-law were hard put to come up with an answer!

Most newlyweds have learned their modes of affection from their mothers. Mom is the one who hugs and says "I love you." Wives often carry two extremes into marriage: a hunger for masculine affection or a fear of it. Husbands find it difficult to express love when they have not observed it in their fathers. The most common complaint about fathers is "I know he loves me, but he never told me so."

Dr. Maurice Prout, speaking of fathers, said, "He probably did more for you and gave you more than you realize. Maybe it wasn't always what you wanted or packaged the way you might have liked, but the gifts were there. The greatest gift of all is the one you may have overlooked: the sense of responsibility in caring for you."[4]

The criticisms heard most frequently in our group about fathers-in-law were "He gives advice to my husband that he doesn't want me to know about" and "He makes me feel like a poor provider by insisting on giving his daughter things he thinks she needs."

Yet sons and daughters are at fault in expecting parents to suddenly quit loving and giving and caring. It is not easy to block out of your life the child to whom you gave birth, nurtured, fed, cried over, prayed for, built dreams around.

Georgie Galbraith, in her "Lines to a Daughter-in-Law," says it beautifully.

Whenever you feel bitter
Toward the mother of your legal lord,
Remember this, my lass:

That she's the lady whose rare qualities,
Whose strength and skill and heart and head
Produced and reared and trained and fed
A small barbaric male
She nursed through measles, mumps and midnight thirst
Into a youth she coaxed and harried
Into that dream of a man you married.[5]

Give your parents a title

How do you put away childish things and, along with your parents, become adults?

Bob Hines, Minister of Adult Education at our church, believes that young marrieds relate better as adults-to-adults if the parents are called by their given names. It is not uncommon for a couple to go for months without addressing their parents-in-law with a name or a title. "My father-in-law is a colonel," said Val, "so I can't call him 'Mister.' And I don't know him well enough to call him 'Dad.'"

Walter said he hadn't had to come up with a title yet, that when he writes to Joan's parents, he begins with "Dear Folks." And when they are all together, he says "Your dad" or "Your mother" if it becomes absolutely necessary to refer to one of them.

"If I called Ben's father 'Dad,' then I'd have two 'Dads,'" said Mary Lou. "I think I'd like to call him by his name, but I'm not sure how he'd feel about it."

Such impasses are two-way. The new son-in-law or daughter-in-law should ask, "What would you like me to call you?" Or the parents should say, "Please call us 'James and Martha,' or 'Mom and Dad.'"

Love, honor, and negotiate

All relationships are built on negotiations. Which, by no means, takes away from the love and honor. Evelyn was about to climb the walls. "As a matter of fact, she did," said Clint. She said she had had it "up to here" with Clint's mother's dropping in at all times of the day or night. She would come by the apartment when Evelyn was at work and clean the kitchen or fold the laundry. "As sure as I sat down to rest or decided to take a nap, in she would walk and, *always*, she'd ask if I were sick. We couldn't call weekends or evenings our own because we never knew when Mom would come by." Clint had difficulty adjusting to the idea of telling his own mother she had to be invited, but finally he did. "Mom was a bit cool for a few days, but she's all right now. We even get anxious to see her between visits." "And she invites us over to her place more," Evelyn added.

Ruth and Kevin's big problem was combining their two families. When they all got together at the same time, they had fireworks or complete silence. After a year and a half of this, Ruth and Kevin came up with a plan of attack. They had private visits with their respective parents and solicited their help. "I told Mom and Dad," said Ruth, "that there was no point in our getting together under the circumstances, that if we could not be congenial, Kevin and I would have to see our parents separately and, that way, they'd see us only half as often. Dad said, 'That would be a sad state of affairs, wouldn't it?' I think they realized then the harm they were doing. Mom and Dad and I didn't argue that day. I just made it clear that Kevin was my number one priority, even though I loved both of them."

We cannot come up with a better pattern than the one Ruth gave us. If there is a problem with *your* parents, it is *your* responsibility to take care of it. If the trouble is with your in-laws, your spouse handles it. And alone. Be sure your parents are assured of your love for them while reminding them that you are a married adult with married adult responsibilities.

Don't blame your parents

You are accountable for your own actions now. To lay your problems at the door of your parents is reverting to childhood.

> "My mother taught me never to leave dirty dishes in the sink."
> "The reason you don't like baseball is because your mother hates sports."
> "Just because your dad sleeps all day Saturday is no excuse for you to."

Stan realized one day that the real reason he wouldn't go with Melinda to the art museum was because his dad had always said such places were "for women and sissies." "When this finally hit me, I got real excited about what I might find in this forbidden place, especially what made Melinda want to go there all the time."

Ask parents' advice

Parents have a storehouse of experience and advice just waiting to be tapped. Also, you honor them with your questions.

Connie stopped by her mother-in-law's office one afternoon because "I had to talk to someone about Neal's battle in trying to find a job. I decided that she, being his mother, was the person most interested in him. I found more help in that short talk with her than I could ever have received from anyone else. Together, we figured out why he was acting so strangely. I learned so much about him. And it made me love her more. We don't live in the same town anymore. But every once in a while, when I don't know what to do, I think of that conversation and it helps me still."

One Thanksgiving morning my mother-in-law received

a phone call from her son and daughter-in-law in California asking for her recipe for sweet potato pudding. That made her day.

"When we bought our car last month," said Clay, "I called my dad to get his opinion. He has been buying cars for years and I knew he knew more about the automobile market than I did."

Share your feelings with your parents

One mother-in-law said, "I never see my daughter-in-law that I do not praise her: her meals, her clothes, her hair, her job. But she has yet to pay me a single compliment."

Why is it so difficult to say "Your recipe is better than mine," "Your roses are bigger," "I like your new suit," "I feel comfortable in your home"? Something good can *always* be found.

Jeanine was extremely uncomfortable with her father- and mother-in-law. Knox had been engaged for two years to a home-town girl whom his parents adored. Jeanine could tell she came in second. "I tried to avoid conversation with them; I felt so grubby when I was around them. Then one evening we went to the theater with Knox's parents and his mother looked absolutely stunning. I told her so. I even told her she had marvelous taste in clothes and that I wished she could pass some of her charm on to me. She said something to the effect that I was a very attractive young woman with a good figure and that she had seen a dress at her boutique that would look great on me. All we needed was an ice-breaker."

Maureen discussed her fears—like death—with her father-in-law. Candy, after a big blow-up at the office where she worked, went straight home and called her mother to get suggestions for handling the next day. Jed and his mother-in-law have great conversations at her kitchen table.

Your parents are people

Parents have problems too. And worries. And fears.

These are the years of the empty nest, retirement, fading health, the fear of death, and living alone. Hopefully, your parents lead busy, happy lives and do not dwell on these changes. But you can be sure they think about them. They may be facing or already are involved in concerns dealing with the health and ages of their parents. They may have problems with your brothers or sisters.

Don't consider them a source of ready cash. Or free baby-sitters. Don't interfere with their schedule or assume they are always available to you. When you go for a meal, help out; take the dessert or salad.

Take your mother to lunch on her birthday.

Buy gifts "just because I thought about you."

Write letters. Send pictures. Go for a drive in the country. Sit with your parents at church.

But, best of all, make time to be together, for unhurried talking—just the two of you.

Families are for sharing

Your brothers and sisters should be your best friends. Your fun times should be more fun with *them*. Your sad times should be more bearable with *them*.

Both Jay and Michelle are "only children." So they adopted, though not legally, Herb and Mary as their brother and sister. "Everyone has such great times with their brothers and sisters," they explained, "and we didn't want to be left out."

Much is written these days on the value of the extended family—and the joys and lessons we miss by no longer living with grandparents, aunts, uncles, and cousins. So, on any occasion available to you to be with relatives, remind yourself that you are adding to your family continuity and helping to fortify your marriage.

Christine says she remembers going to a family reunion when she was a teenager, pouting all the way, and her mother saying, "You are going to meet some relatives you never saw, which will mean more to you than staying at home and going swimming. You have precious few kinfolks as it is and it's my duty to see that you get to know them." Christine said it was weird logic to her at the time, but now "I see the benefit of relatives. That must mean I'm growing up."

In *Families*, Jane Howard confirms the value of the extended family when she writes, "Too much privacy and we won't have anyone with whom to remember, let alone with whom to make plans. Too much individualism and we forget not only our ancestors and our possible descendants but even each other."[6]

DISCUSSION STARTERS

1. What do you call your mother-in-law? Father-in-law?

2. What characteristics do you see in your father-in-law (or mother-in-law) that you also see in your spouse?

3. What attracted you to your mate? Do you see this quality in either of his/her parents?

4. Do you fit into the "complementary sibling roles" described by Dr. Toman? If so, how has this helped you?

5. What do you learn from brothers and sisters that helps you in your marriage?

6. What is the most common criticism you receive from your mother or mother-in-law? Father or father-in-law? Put on cards and compile. Then ask, "Are these legitimate complaints?"

7. What do you think would be the most difficult thing about being a mother-in-law? Father-in-law?

8. What is the most difficult part of being a daughter-in-law? Son-in-law?

9. Have a role-playing session in which parent-and-child or parents-and-children situations are acted out. Use the following examples or make up your own:

(1) A son calls his father to tell him he and his wife can't visit him this summer, that they are taking a trip to the West Coast instead. (How does the father feel? Does he say what he thinks? What do you expect him to say? Suppose you were in *his* place?)

(2) The two couples are having dinner at the newlyweds' house. The young husband asks his mother to give his wife the recipe for this favorite dish of his. The wife says, "I have a recipe for that." (Note the mother's reaction. What should the wife have said? Was the husband upbraiding his wife by asking for his mother's recipe?)

(3) The mother, who is a spotless housekeeper, goes to visit her daughter, who obviously is a poor housekeeper. The mother says something like "I feel terribly guilty about all this. I feel it is my fault you can't keep house properly. I should have taken more time to teach you." (Note the daughter's reaction. What should the mother do when she sees the house in shambles?)

6

COMMUNICATION

"I couldn't say 'hello.' Just as I couldn't say 'goodbye' or 'thank you' or even 'I love you' unless the setting was just right."

This was Carl, assuming blame for the awkward style of conversation in the early part of his marriage.

"For the first six months, Gail left in the mornings before I did. Responding to her goodbyes was simple enough. And when I returned home in the afternoons, it was always Gail who was first with the 'Hi, how are you?' or 'Did you have a good day?'

"Then a month ago our schedules changed and I had to leave for an early class before Gail left for work. I just couldn't do the farewell routine. I'd slink out the door with a weak 'see ya' or make with a clumsy kiss.

"Gail sensed my problem and insisted we talk about it. Way into the night we talked. I wonder if I would ever have been rid of this hang-up if Gail had not seen through me."

Carl's parents had always talked in questions. "Are you leaving?" "Are you ready to eat?" "When did you buy that dress?" There was no ritual about departures or arrivals, no formal gift-giving, no show of affection. So Carl's new task in communication involves unlearning as well as learning. Adult communication habits are not easy to change. Gail's sensitivity was the solution to what could have been an impasse.

Jim said, "My problem was much like that. I'd go in to breakfast and never say a word. I'm a real mute when I first wake up in the mornings. Finally we hit upon the simple plan that I would say 'good morning' as I walked into the kitchen, and Polly promised not to speak to me before that."

Becky said her dad had a special tune he whistled as he walked down the hall every morning. The family recognized it as "I'm up and ready for the day; I'm also ready for breakfast."

Dr. Dan Bagby, pastor of Seventh and James Baptist Church, Waco, Texas, says that his father, when he wanted to announce that he was home and available to his family, would play the piano.

Good questions

Obviously, questions are necessary for communicating. Good questions promote conversation, while poor ones lead to a dead end.

Instead of asking, "Did you have a good day?" try, "What did Mr. Wilson say when you explained your reorganization plan?" A question like "Did you win?" or "Did you buy the new dress?" requires nothing more than a "yes" or "no." "How did the scoring go?" and "What kind of dresses are in style this fall?" are likely to initiate conversations. The person who complains that "you don't talk to me" often is the one who uses the "yes" and "no" questions.

Wise timing

When we hear the phrase "poor timing," most of us conjure up this picture of the wife bombarding the husband with problems as soon as he walks in the door from work. Yet, there are worse times. Sarah learned this the hard way. If Ron talked too much at a party, Sarah could hardly wait to get in the car to lecture him. She complained in the presence of his friends when he came home late from playing tennis. When he was in a romantic mood, she considered it a safe time to tell him about the insurance bill she forgot to pay or the possibility that they'd miss the boat trip because her sister was coming into town. Finally Sarah's gregarious, loving husband had become a somber stranger.

Sarah's tactics were deflating to Ron. When this was pointed out to her, she learned to wait until the next day to criticize. By then she was less agitated and usually decided to say nothing.

"I learned about timing," said David, "in one grand swoop! We were having friends in for dinner. We'd been married only a few weeks, and Karen was still learning to cook. She always got a little nervous about entertaining. Well, she was in the kitchen putting bread crumbs on a zucchini casserole. I said 'I hate zucchini.' She walked to the sink, dumped the whole thing in the garbage disposal, said, 'Okay, master chef, the kitchen's all yours,' and stormed out of the room. Needless to say, we didn't have a casserole for dinner."

Karen admits she overreacted, but David learned. He never again complained of her menu choices before or during a meal.

Many a marriage has been saved by the practice of wise timing.

Talking seriously

Some husbands and wives have the same difficulty in initiating a serious conversation that Carl had in saying hello. "I'd get up my nerve to say 'Let's talk,'" said Anne, "and Rick would respond with 'About what?' When I tried to give a title to my important subject, it became unimportant. If you want to talk about feelings and things like that, you don't want to make an announcement. What I really mean when I say I want to talk is to explain and share; I want it to be a sort of crescendo. It always ended up that we didn't talk at all. My solution came from something I read on one of those sentimental cards I saw in a gift shop that said 'I want to tell you how I love you.' That night when Rick answered 'About what?' I said 'About how much I love you.' This got his attention *and* his interest."

If Rick had been more sensitive to Anne's needs (which might have required his putting down his newspaper or turning off the TV), these hand-in-hand talks could have been a part of their relationship from the beginning.

Overcommunication

Then there are those who talk too much, who are over-communicators. Cindy, even now, is a chatterbox. In fact, her indestructible gift of gab was what attracted Kent to her in college. She ran interference for him; she was his social security. But now he was working for a law firm, where he felt besieged by words from 8:00 to 5:00. He would have liked tranquility at home, but he knew the minute he opened the door Cindy would begin a barrage of words that would run on all evening. "Finally I got the picture," said Cindy, "and started working on zipping my lip. But it wasn't easy. In the middle of one of my elaborations once, I stopped and said, 'I'm trying, Kent, I really am trying.' And he said, 'I'm trying too.' That's when I knew he was making a special effort to be more open. We're still working at helping each other. It isn't easy for either of us, but it's more enjoyable."

Kent and Cindy's communication patterns were part of their divergent personalities. But these patterns were also results of habits. We develop these speech habits in childhood and carry them with us into adulthood. It is by being aware of this and working at it that we bring about changes. And most of us have to have these problems pointed out to us.

Giving and getting the message

It was one of those frequent misunderstandings between Jack and Carrie. They usually dismissed these sessions as breakdowns in communication. But this one proved too serious to take lightly. It happened when Jack said he'd like to take the next Friday off from work and have a long weekend at the family lake house. Carrie said she doubted that she could get off. Jack said, "Well, you could try." Carrie talked to her boss the next day and got permission to use one of her vacation days. When she told Jack that night, he blew his top. "Carrie, that was stupid, real stupid! I didn't tell you to ask for a day off. I just said I *wished* we could go to the lake Friday. There's no way I could leave then."

Having to endure the embarrassment of retracting her request with her supervisor gave Carrie the impetus to take action at home. She and Jack learned to ask "What do you mean?" "What do you want me to do?" "Will you please explain that?" Like many married couples, they had been assuming instead of asking.

Overintensifying

Wives, more than husbands, overintensify. They often exaggerate to get attention or to drive a point home or to rationalize actions or feelings. Like Doris. Hank had learned that she was never as sick or as tired or as busy as she would have him believe. She was like the boy who yelled "wolf." So Hank became oblivious to her complaints. Even in legitimate situations, he brushed aside her pleas for help. When Doris realized that Hank did not respond the way her parents and her roommates had, she learned to present a true picture. Consequently, she became a more contented person. So did Hank.

Often negativism is an ingredient of overintensifying. And sometimes it's simply that one is a negative person. That habit *can* be changed.

Friends called Sally and Steve "Sun and Moon." Sally was cheerful, optimistic, and congenial. Steve was gloomy, pessimistic and disbelieving. If Sally said, "It's a beautiful day," Steve would say, "The humidity is terrible." If she related a good experience with a friend at work, he would say, "She's trying to use you." When she congratulated herself on cleaning the hall closet, he said, "You should have done that months ago." One day a neighbor asked Sally, "Is he always so unhappy?" Sally repeated this to Steve. He didn't tell Sally, but he began to look at himself in light of the neighbor's question. He reasoned that his attitude would be destructive in his profession as well as in his marriage and his friendships. Becoming a Positive when you've been a Negative all your life is no easy matter. But Steve is enjoying the challenge and, for the first time, admits that he's beginning to like himself.

Comfortable communication with each other

Why is it that husbands and wives who have difficulty talking with each other can talk for hours with friends? This is a common question asked of counselors. Wives say that three-fourths of what they know about their husbands they learn from listening to the husbands' conversations with other people. Husbands complain that their wives spend an entire evening in female chatter and can't tell their husbands a thing they've talked about. One husband said that in order to talk with his wife the way he does with his friends he'd have to give her a briefing of his daily activities. He said she wouldn't understand his references or innuendos or jokes and probably wouldn't appreciate them if she did. The wife said, "Why didn't you ever explain it to me like that?" He had not bothered to sift through his activities and feelings and give her the highlights even, a method that would have been more than acceptable to her.

Ellen was really afraid to share her feelings with Bob. As likely as not he would say, "That's silly" or, "You're making a mountain out of a molehill" or, "You're cluttering your mind." Or he'd turn her off by walking away or watching the TV. So if he asks, "What did you two talk about?" she says, "Nothing," and he becomes exasperated.

Our feelings are as much a part of our lives as are our activities. We should feel free to share both.

Ideas on communication strategy

A brainstorming of ideas on communication strategy gives us this list:

Have a signal to indicate "I'm listening to you," such as lifting your finger or stroking your chin.

Create a "conversation bank," a list of topics to share, one a day, with your spouse. (You may even want to write them in a notebook.)

Along the same line, read. Know what's going on around you; be interested and interesting.

One night a week (preferably the same night each week) keep the TV turned off.

Use the word "we" instead of "you" whenever possible. "We" forgot to lock the door, instead of "you" forgot to lock the door. "We" are spending too much money. "We" should wake up earlier.

Remember that you may be married to a person who

communicates by *doing:* frying chicken for dinner because it's your favorite food, warming the car for you on cold mornings, suggesting that you invite your friends for the evening.

"We don't talk to each other" is a common complaint of couples in the middle years of marriage. Counselors tell us these patterns are set early, probably during the first few months together.

Good communication, nurtured, kept current and cherished, can save a marriage. But, more than that, as Emerson said, it can give your love its "sabbaths and jubilees."[1]

DISCUSSION STARTERS

1. On the chalkboard or a posterboard put a statement or question such as "I knew you'd do that" or "Where have you been so long?" Ask: "What is the meaning?" (show that the message is determined by *how* we say what we say.)

2. How do we communicate without words?
(Silence, smile, gestures, wink, clearing throat, whistle, shrugging shoulders, turning away, etc.)

3. Explain the idea, espoused by certain therapists, that men and women *listen* differently.
(Most men pay more attention to the substance of a conversation than to its process; most women respond to its process.)

4. Have the following monologues read aloud by a wife (number one) and a husband (number two), asking the group to listen for the real message.

   NUMBER ONE: "The Stevensons down the street are going to be moving next week. . . . Oh, you know them. . . . Louise walks her dog in the afternoons often when I walk Pepper. We went to that art show together last week, remember? She said then that she was afraid they would be moving to St. Louis, that Joe expected to be transferred there, even though they have lived here such a short time. Louise is a marvelous cook. She gave me that recipe for Swiss steak you like so much. We were planning to make fruit-cakes together for Christmas. . . . All of this means we're going to have a house for sale on our street and, eventually, a new family moving in."

NUMBER TWO: "Do you know that John Carter sold those golf clubs of his to Mel Jones yesterday? He didn't even ask me if I'd like to have them. I told him several months ago, when he was talking about get-ting some new ones, that I'd like to buy his old ones. And he knew his old ones were better than mine; we talked about it the last time we played together."

5. Choose a couple to talk five minutes on a given subject (events of the day, upcoming trip, letter from home, etc.). Ask one person privately to keep a list of *questions* used in the conversation, another, a list of *statements*. Compare.

7

FIGHTING

The first fight is the shocker.

"The first time I heard Amy scream, I couldn't believe it was Amy," said Russell. "I was in such a state of shock, actually, that I forgot what we were arguing about and couldn't even strike back."

Regardless of disagreements and spats before marriage, the real knock-down-drag-out usually comes after the honeymoon. Housekeeping has begun, meals have been burned, the alarm clock has failed to ring, and the garbage has piled up. Courtship was never like this.

Results of questionnaires to seventy-five couples in our groups showed the ten leading causes of arguments among newlyweds to be these:

1. Lateness
2. Money
3. Household chores
4. Cooking (meals)
5. In-laws
6. Roles
7. Recreation (leisure time)
8. Untidiness
9. Lack of communication
10. Work

After the initial brawl, Russell realized he no longer held the reins. "In college, I could make with the dramatics and the only exchange I'd get from the men was physical. I kicked doors and threw shoes, but no one ever *screamed* at me."

Youth has volatile emotions, seldom harnessed before the twenties. When two spirited young people unite these fervors, explosions usually result. So becoming fair in love and war is a learning—and practicing—process.

Home influences play a big role in the reasons for and methods of marital fighting. For example, you learned tactics from your parents without being aware of it. Possibly you are a child whose demands were met without battles, or you may have brought into marriage unidentifiable fears.

Doyle's retort to Cora when she displeased him was "That's not logical." "I was so tired of hearing that word," said Cora. "If I had believed him, it would have taken me about one week to decide that I was a real lame brain. Everything I did was illogical. Finally I started throwing the word back at him. 'Doyle, that's not logical.' Eventually, it passed out of our vocabulary."

Lou Ann would not consider making any changes in her behavior. Her response was always, "That's the way I am" or, "You know how I am, so don't push me." She expected Art to give in to her simply because *her* pattern was set. One night Art asked her, "If *you* don't change and *I* don't change, how are we going to make it?" A compromise was in order.

Change is possible

We *can* change. We *can* rid ourselves of temper tantrums, stubbornness, dogmatism, and retaliation, the four major elements of family feuds.

Rita came from a family of shouters and table-bangers, whereas Ned's parents always went into their bedroom to air their differences, out of ear range of Ned and his brother. Therefore, Rita's surprise came not in the fact of fighting, but in the absence of it. "I really like to get a problem out in the open and get it over with," she said. "I like the confrontation. But Ned shies away from it." When Rita learns to hold her tongue more and Ned learns to loosen his, both will be in healthier situations.

"The last time I had an argument at home," said Colleen, "my mother said to me, 'Colleen, if you can't get along with us here, how do you expect to get along with a husband?' I started to say, 'Well, he won't be as mean to me as all of you are' or something like that. But then I realized that wasn't true; he might be worse. That kind of scared me into changing my ways."

If we could recognize them, we'd see our fears surface in our quarrels.

Much like Ned, Mary Ann avoided entanglements. But when she finally did get angry, she would yell at Dow, "Don't tell me what to do; I'm a grown woman, remember?" Yet around her parents she reverted to a little girl. She was afraid that if she ever let Dow take charge of her, he, like her parents, would reduce her to a child.

It took Lori a long time to solve the mystery of Rudy's blowups. It seemed to happen often when she would praise him or compliment him. Then once, as a form of apology, he said, "I'm always afraid you're trying to manipulate me. Just like people have done all my life." Rudy's family had used praise to get him to do what they wanted. He anticipated that marriage would bring a freedom from these schemes.

If your weapon causes irritation to your mate, try something new. And better.

Looking at yourself

Do you see yourself in these complaints?

"He is *always* right. He even *says* so. 'Oh, you are wrong; you are *so* wrong.' Or 'I'm right, I'm right.'"

"She asks me to make the phone call, then she stands there and tells me what to say."

"She always has a legitimate excuse for everything she does wrong."

"He always expects the worst from me, so when it happens, he says, 'I told you so.'"

"He says, 'Shut up.' He is the only person who has *ever* said 'Shut up' to me."

"She getsry because I won't talk to her. Here I am, haven't said a word, and she gets mad."

"He laughs at me."

"She never apologizes."

"He has a way of turning everything around and blaming *me* because *he* got sore."

In every marriage there should be *Ground Rules for Fighting.* Here are some our classes recommend.

Make allowances for circumstances

Maybe she's tired. Or sick. Someone chewed him out at the office. She's worried about her family. His friend didn't invite him to play golf.

In *The Home: Laboratory of Life,* John Drakeford describes three types of emotional discords in marriage: dated emotions, displaced emotions, drained emotions. Dated emotions are those that were normal in childhood, but are inadequate for adults. Displaced ones are illustrated in the proverbial story of the husband, chastised by his boss, who goes home and yells at his wife. Drained emotions we know about. Pent-up feelings must be released. Talking, crying, sobbing are safety valves well understood by the average newlywed.[1]

Keep the subject current

Don't bring up the past. "When I make a mistake," said

Joyce, "Dean makes it seem like just another in a long string of failures. 'You did this same thing last week.' 'Just like you always do.' 'When are you going to learn?'"

"I think I want her to have a surplus," explained Dean, "so that when *I* goof, she won't say anything."

Keep it private

Lucy needs a sounding board for her gripes. Most of her darts are thrown at Pete in public—a self-defeating ploy. The sympathy of family and friends is with Pete.

The people at the office get frequent reports of the latest fracas at the Adams house. Jerry hasn't learned the husbandly art of keeping it inside his own four walls.

Declare no winners

Never, never should a winner be declared in the battle of husband and wife.

In the words of Ogden Nash,

> To keep your marriage brimming
> With love in the loving cup,
> Whenever you're wrong, admit it;
> When you're right, shut up.[2]

Separate fighting and love-making

Margo learned about sexual accuations from her friend Norma. Periodically Norma would get on a talking spree and complain that her husband considered belittling their sex life his strongest form of insult. "I couldn't believe people did such things," said Margo. "But Norma says it's a problem with several people she knows. Can you imagine?"

No, we can't. But it happens. And with dreadful results. Few marriages can survive it.

Always bring your argument to conclusion

We are admonished in Ephesians 4:26, "Let not the sun go down on your wrath." So when you go to bed, be sure the argument is put to rest too.

That means bring it to a conclusion. End it. Get it out of the way. Kill it. Fights that go on and on and on cause ulcers and headaches and sleepless nights and bad days at the office. Don't wait until you go to bed; end it quickly. Never leave an argument dangling.

Roy's way of ending a dispute was to walk off, which actually added fuel. Sharon became angry because he wouldn't stay and fight. Roy not only was taking the easy way out, he was showing a lack of concern for Sharon.

"We came up with our own ground rule," said Gina. "We agreed to allow each other five minutes to give our reasons for being mad. And during that five minutes, the other one could not interrupt with questions or motions or anything. The best thing we got rid of this way was my usual 'I'm sorry, I'm sorry.' Before Jesse could get started, I'd stymie him by breaking in with an apology meant solely to hush him."

Eliminate blaming words

Some words close the door on hearing both sides of an argument. Look out for these:

Never. "You *never* let me know when you're going to be late."
Always. "You *always* say that."
You think. "*You think* I'm stupid."
You forget. "*You forget* the time *you* ran out of gas."
You believe. "*You believe* your dad is smarter than mine."
We can't tell other people what they think or forget or

believe. Only as they pertain to us can we properly use these words in statements. To use them in questions ("Do you think?" "Did you forget?" "Do you believe?") is quite a different matter.

Be honest

Be sure you know why you are angry. Level with your spouse. Are you mad at the traffic or the situation at hand? Say what you are really feeling. "I'm worried about that insurance policy you forgot to pay" instead of "I'm disgusted with you for being so unorganized."

Also, it doesn't hurt to begin your tirade with "I love you even though—"

After this idea was suggested, Darrell and Molly decided to try it for the next week. They reported that every time they began a tongue-lashing with "I love you even though you—," that's as far as they'd get; they'd break up in laughter.

Which leads us to

Try humor

This doesn't mean laugh at. Or even smile at. Nelda said, "I hate it when I'm upset and I'm trying to make a point and Ralph sits over there with a silly smile on his face. I know what I'm saying is not at all important to him."

The incidents with Darrell and Molly, however, are examples of humor used constructively.

Laughter ended an argument for Pat and Liza when Liza remembered the class discussion on the rules for fighting. "Now, Pat, we're not doing this right; we're forgetting the rules."

(You can buy from some gift shops and department

stores a punching pillow called a "love bat." Try that for getting rid of some irritations and adding fun to your anger.)

Argue only about things that can be resolved

There is no point in screaming about the weather or the test you have to take tomorrow. If it's already too late to get your clothes from the cleaners, lambasting each other won't help.

Dr. Joyce Brothers, in an undated article in my collection, explains her way of handling such frustrations. "When I get in a bad mood, it doesn't last long because I can usually locate the real source of my irritation and do something positive about it. If I have no control over the situation, then I try to accept that fact and write it off."[3]

Never leave scars

This is the big one. Like the insults on sex activity, some scars are so deep they never disappear. They are always in the subconscious as a reminder of a black day.

Avoid accusations.

Don't leave home.

Don't dominate.

Don't be physical.

Count to ten. Or twenty. Or thirty.

If your problem is too big for you, get professional help.

But *don't leave scars*. Remember, words once spoken cannot be taken back.

Creative arguing

There *are* advantages to constructive fighting.

Critiquing your argument together can reveal your

weaknesses. And strengths. What to get rid of and what to hold on to.

Problems are brought out in the open, where they can be dealt with.

Robb had his office at home. Betsy worked downtown. She had reached a point where she was never sure how to greet Robb when she came home in the afternoons: to say hello and take the chance of his growling back, or ignore him and hurt his feelings. So one day she came home with a big red hat for Robb to wear when he is in a bad mood!

Constructive arguing can bring about a release from tension. It can clear muddled minds. It can help give significance to the lull.

Then there's the "making up!"

A current magazine ad reads, "Imagine tomorrow without argument. How disagreeable." The ad goes on to say argument "clears the air, opens up minds to conflicting ideas, makes proud intellectuals and ordinary folks ask themselves if their cherished assumptions are based on real knowledge or prejudice, fashion, or rote response."[4]

So it is with marriage.

DISCUSSION STARTERS

1. When you were growing up, which parent did most of the talking? Which one made most of the decisions? (Talk doesn't always mean action.)

2. Surveys (on unsigned cards):
   What is the subject of most of your arguments?
   When do most of your arguments take place?
   Where? (In car, kitchen, bedroom, etc.)
   Why? (Tired, rushed, sick, uptight, worried, etc.)

3. What irritates you? Why?

4. List some constructive ways of releasing your anger. (Is it necessary to get angry in the first place?)

5. What characteristics of fighting did you bring from your childhood into your marriage?

6. Name some fears that are often involved in marital fighting.

7. How can an argument be ended without someone's winning?

8. Do you agree with the maxim "Never let the sun go down on your wrath"?

9. List (on cards) words that need to be eliminated in *your* arguments.

10. List some ways in which a family fight can be constructive.

11. Originate or secure (from counselors, experiences, etc.) four or five case histories of husband-and-wife fighting patterns. Discuss what causes their anger. What changes should be made?

12. Role-playing. Dramatize situations in this chapter or from your own and group members' imaginations and knowledge.

8

MONEY

To drink from the eyes of a woman who is a perfect
fountain of delight, to feel the doors of Paradise opened to
us by her lips; and then all at once to be obliged to speak of
income amidst such intoxicating pleasures; it is hard, cruel,
abominable—but it is necessary!

—Vico Mantegazza[1]

Panic is a common motivator for financial planning in
young marriages. Only after the elusive dollar has
brought us to our knees—which usually comes in the
third or fourth month—do we settle down with pen and
yellow pad to assess the damage and plan ahead, to
discredit the adage that two can live as cheaply as one.

Robert had a sneaky feeling that he and Claire would
have money problems. While they were in college, she
wore expensive clothes, served steaks when they cooked
at her apartment, and had charge accounts all over town.
But she was sure she would be able to control her urge to
splurge once they were settled in and living on their two
meager incomes. But habits and long-standing attitudes
are hard to change. Claire overextended her credit by
spending the usual amount for gifts. She bought groceries
at the local quick-stop store instead of the supermarket.
She was oblivious to the extra charge for long-distance
phone calls. She strongly believed that "you get what you
pay for." Especially in clothes. "I really believe," she said,

"that *one good* dress is better than *three cheap* ones." But four "good" dresses in three months?

It was at the end of this third month that Claire and Robert took the first realistic look at their income and outgo. They had received threatening letters from creditors. Robert had had to borrow money from his folks to pay the rent. "We didn't even have money for a movie," said Claire. They learned the hard way that a budget is essential. They pooled their bank accounts, paid cash for all expenditures, and kept track of every check and every purchase.

Howard Hovde, in *The Neo-Married*, says good attitudes about money are vital to the success of a marriage; they "are likely to carry over into many other decisions."[2]

People like Claire can change habits quickly, while their philosophy on spending dies a slow death or hangs in limbo. Otherwise, the result will be heavy-sledding—for the financial program and for the marriage.

Separate funds

Yet every husband and wife *should have individual funds*, an allowance to spend without giving account. No one should be reduced to the position of beggar by having to plead for money.

"We argued constantly about money," said Charlotte. "I was in school, not working, and contributing nothing to the family income. I had to ask Brent for every penny I spent, including school lunches. My only source of private funds was my lunch money. So I started taking my lunch, using dinner leftovers. When Brent learned about this, he took even the lunch money away, saying the homemade lunches were a good idea, that we could *save* the cash he'd been giving me."

At this point Charlotte went into a period of depression that led to the need for psychotherapy. The counselor suggested to Brent that, along with other changes, he open a private checking account for Charlotte, put in it a specified amount each month for household expenses and personal spending—with no questions asked.

"I don't have to beg for money anymore," says Charlotte, "or hide what I've bought or think of an explanation. It's great!"

And, for the first time, the marriage is on solid ground. So solid, in fact, that Charlotte, even though she has now graduated from college, has opted to remain at home as a full-time housewife.

Rules for paying the bills

When I was six years old I memorized a poem.

> When Ma gets out the monthly bills
> And sets them all in front of Dad,
> She makes us children run and play
> Because she knows he might get mad.

"This is our evening to pay bills" usually carries with it a message of anticipated calamity. The dread can be lessened somewhat by adhering to a few decided-ahead-of-time rules.

Keep the date.
If you decide to pay bills on the first day of the month, or the 10th or the 15th, let nothing short of an emergency interfere. If you have plans for that night (or day), settle the accounts the night before, not the night after.

Select a payer.
Joel thought it was the man's duty to pay the bills. But he procrastinated. Carolyn fussed so much that in a moment of anger, Joel suggested that she take over the job.

For Carolyn it was no big deal. "I spend an hour or so once a month—and that's it." Joel is so relieved that he isn't even embarrassed to tell people that his wife pays the bills.

Annette, who works half-days, takes care of bills as soon as they arrive. There is no "bill-paying" night. "For me, it's easier to do a little every day rather than a big stack once a month."

Vic and Shannon work together on bills. He writes the checks; she addresses the envelopes, stuffs them, and stamps them. "This way we *both* know what we're spending."

Agree on changes.

When additional economy is needed, share in the cutback. We are told that the average family allots approximately 15 percent of its total income to discretionary spending. From that portion, you can make the decision as to what to cut. Don't assume the extra money you need *has* to come out of the grocery money or transportation expenses; maybe you should cut down on recreation or meals out.

Keep an emergency fund.

For illness, a trip home, automobile repairs, even a new dress required for a special party.

Make major purchases together.

Never surprise your mate by pulling up in the driveway with a new car or bringing home the antique chest you just couldn't live without. Secret purchases should be limited to gifts.

Borrow from the bank.

If it becomes necessary to float a loan, go to a bank or a loan company. Only in rare circumstances should you borrow from relatives or friends. Getting your dad to co-sign a note with you is quite acceptable.

Living on less

Somewhere along the line, you may have to start living on one income. Don't crater.

"We thought we had reached the living end when I got pregnant and had to quit work," said Kim. "But we tightened the traces and made it. We found that we saved a great deal of money by my staying home. I cut my clothes budget way down. (Not having to buy panty hose every week helps.) No more bus fares, downtown lunches, with-the-crowd shopping. I saved on our food bills by doing planned marketing once a week. I had time to sew. I even wrote letters instead of making long distance phone calls."

Consider also the tax impact of combining two salaries. How else to stretch the dollar?

First of all, *keep records.*

Vernon and I have among our souveniers our first household ledger, the only week's entry showing an unreconciled loss of five cents. We hope you will do better. John Bloskas's very practical book *Staying in the Black Financially* includes a sample financial record for young couples.[3] Use it, or work up your own, but keep the spending down in black and white.

Beware of shopping temptations.

The freedom of using the credit card tops the list of temptations. Possibly you went off to college with two or three family credit cards to use for handy shopping; paying in cash became awkward. It is easy to be swayed by the commercial sales pitches that engulf us, not only for using credit cards, but for buying on time. Do not be intimidated. Discuss purchases. Make rational decisions. Glow in the fact of living within your income.

A recent profile of young couples with overextended credit showed these common characteristics:

(1) average-size incomes,
(2) weak will power,
(3) unorganized households,
(4) lack of savings and emergency funds,
(5) no budget,
(6) fondness for watching TV.

Know your friendly grocer.

Reuben Herring tells about his son who, while living at home, had been an impetuous consumer of bacon. After marriage, his assessment of housekeeping was the outrageous price of bacon![4]

Comparative shopping, meal planning, regular and infrequent trips to the store can make a big difference in food bills. Find a convenient, good supermarket and get to know it. And its manager. Buy sale items, but only if you use them. Likewise with coupon offers. Plan your meals and shop once a week. My father-in-law likes to tell of the time he opened a charge account with a neighborhood grocer. With three children available to go to the store, the first month's bill was made up of thirty-six charges!

Many working couples stop for groceries on the way home from work and are influenced by both lack of time and an appetite. Economists say *never shop for food when you are hungry.* You buy the wrong items and too many of them.

As you put your groceries away, check each item on your ticket. Everyone makes mistakes, even supermarket checkers. It is when you find mistakes in your bill or when you have to return imperfect items that you benefit from knowing the store personnel.

You may want to join a neighborhood vegetable and fruit co-op. Or plant a garden. Or freeze foods in season. Definitely you want to learn to use leftovers.

Dolores was anxious for us to know that, *for free*, you can check out paintings, tapes, and records at large public libraries—and not have to spend money on those luxuries right now. "Besides, with the paintings, you can decide what you want when you do get enough money for such things."

The big expenses

Then come the big, big decisions. Whether to continue your education. Or both your educations. To buy a house or rent an apartment.

If you plan to get a college degree, now is the time. It is easy to get started in the business world, then find it difficult to break away and go back to school. Often wives choose to work so that their husbands can pursue graduate degrees. Great caution is needed. Statistics show that by the time husbands complete their advanced programs, marriages often are on the rocks. The wife has not kept pace with her husband intellectually and socially. "My mother kept warning me about that," said Nellie. "Periodically she'd ask, 'Nellie, are you sure you're not letting Grant get ahead of you?' Or she'd suggest that maybe I should go back to school too. She's a college teacher and she has seen so many marriages break up this way. She never let me relax until Grant finished his degree and she saw that our marriage was still intact."

Loans and scholarships are available for continued education. Often parents agree to help with tuition. So if both of you want to go to school, you probably can.

Most young couples do not like to see the bulk of their income spent for apartment rent. So as soon as the first job is obtained, the dream of owning a house begins to surface. The couple find themselves shackled to a mortgage that requires two salaries and frequent help from parents. Advice from home-owners and financial experts is in order. Keep in mind that you are buying not just a house. "We were unprepared for the amount we had to spend just to start living in our house," said Olivia. "We had to buy a lawn mower and a ladder and yard tools. Besides buying grass and shrubbery. During the first year we had a big repair bill on our air conditioning and several plumbing bills. The real estate agent didn't tell us about all that."

Luxuries

Someone has said, "Share luxuries but don't keep count." What is a luxury? We asked in our groups, What is your number one luxury? The top answers:

1. Eating out.
2. Vacations.
3. Automobile(s) (and trips).
4. Stereo equipment.
5. Recreation and entertainment.
6. Good clothes.
7. Furniture.

Never did television appear on these lists, though everyone has a TV. Never the word "pets," though approximately half have dogs or cats at home. Our neighborhood veterinarian estimates the cost of owning a healthy dog at two hundred to four hundred dollars a year, depending, of course, upon the breed of dog. So if you are counting pennies, think twice about pets. Hobbies such as golf, tennis, photography, painting, even raising house plants have played havoc with budgets. Be sure you don't confuse hobbies with necessities.

Giving, together

When Bob and Marguerite married thirty years ago, he was a medical student and they were living on her salary. The first Sunday morning after they moved into their apartment, Marguerite found Bob at the desk writing a check for a tenth of her salary—their tithe to the church. "Here, I, who had given my dime-a-Sunday for all of my twenty-three years, suddenly was giving a tenth of my salary every Sunday!" The adjustment was not easy, but Marguerite is quick to tell you it was the only way. To expect to build up to it or find an appropriate time would have been a delusion.

Do not let your money make you a Scrooge. Enjoy giving *together*.

Luke's mother died last year. She was a patron of the symphony orchestra in their hometown. She helped to raise money to get out publicity, to bring the best guest artists to perform. "It was so important to her," said Luke, "that I find my greatest solace in giving money to help support her symphony."

Gordon and Dorothy help every year with the Christmas party for underprivileged children. They pick several youngsters up at their homes and take them to the party. They help decorate the tree and bake cookies. But, best of all, "we buy two rather expensive gifts, one for a boy, one for a girl. It's the most fun we have all year: choosing the toys, watching the little faces light up, hearing the squeals. And it's the very best thing we do with our money."

Your money can increase your scope of influence,

spread your love and add to your fun, as well as provide for the necessities of life.

And, on the subject of *things,* materialistic possessions, take it from Dr. Dobson, author of *What Wives Wish Their Husbands Knew About Women:* "I can tell you they don't deliver the satisfaction they advertise! On the contrary, I have found great wisdom in the adage 'that which you own will eventually own you.'"[5]

DISCUSSION STARTERS

1. How does your childhood influence your adult attitude toward money?

2. Pass out sheets from a budget book or make copies of Bloskas's record (*Staying in the Black Financially*, p. 20) or Hovde's sample budget (*The Neo-Married*, p. 45). Give couples ten minutes to fill in categories, using percentages rather than figures (10 percent of the salary here, 5 percent here, etc.).

3. List on chalkboard answers to the questions, "What do you consider the main cause of insufficient funds when both husband and wife are working?" Discuss.

4. On page 38 of Herring's *Building a Better Marriage* is the statement "The couple that cannot manage on $5,000 a year cannot manage on $10,000 or even $50,000." Do you agree?

5. What are the advantages and disadvantages of credit cards? Time payments?

6. If you needed a loan, would you borrow from your father? Why? Why not?

7. If your income were cut in half, what changes would you make in your life style?

8. Share ideas and tricks for economizing on the food bill.

9. Which is more feasible for the average newly married, recently employed couple: renting an apartment or buying a house? Possibly two people can debate this. How does a couple know when the time is right for buying a house?

10. Compile the answers to: "What is your number one luxury?"

11. What is the most unselfish thing you do with your money?

9

TIME

My sister-in-law Mildred complained of not having enough time. So her four teenagers got together and voted her 26-hour days!

Most of us, even with two extra hours each day, would not have enough time. Yet, in this one aspect of our lives, we are all equals. No amount of talent or brains or planning will give us longer or shorter days than those of anyone else.

Periodically, everyone needs restoration, a change of scenery, relief from cabin fever. But how?

Take a walk. Spend an entire evening in conversation with a friend. Get carried away with a good book. Laugh. Cry. Pray. Back off and get things in perspective. If you can manage it, take a vacation, for a weekend or a week. Kenneth Chafin suggests that husbands and wives reverse roles on vacations. Whatever rejuvenates *you* will help you to make better—and more enjoyable—use of your time.

When you're always late

Bill Cosby says the difference between old people and young people is that old people are always on time. Psychologists often describe habitually tardy adults as being "adolescent" because they still are rebelling against authority, having transferred the relationship with their parents to a relationship with the clock!

So if you are on the time merry-go-round—never gaining, always losing, always late—you are *stealing* time, from yourself as well as from others. Surveys on the major problems of young marrieds always list near the top the battle with *time:* the use of it, the lack of it.

"We don't do a lot of things now," said Stacy, "because we just don't have time. We know that later on we'll have time to do what we want."

Not so. You will never have enough time. (Only Mildred has 26-hour days!) Marriage and family counselor Dr. Tom Bourne suggests you answer these three questions when attempting to improve your life, time-wise (or marriage-wise):

1. How do you use your *time?*
2. How do you use your *space?*
3. How do you use your *energy?* [1]

If you are late for work, you steal time from your boss. If you are late to a party, you steal from your hostess. If you are a piddler or a foot-dragger or a messer, you steal from your spouse. And from you.

Lee had three alarm clocks in his room at school, "besides a loud roommate," and he still had trouble waking up in the mornings. So it was only fitting that he turn over the responsibility for the wake-up call to Phyllis. The problem was that Phyllis was a zombie too.

"First of all, we started going to bed earlier at night," said Phyllis, "and that helped a little. But the real clincher came when Lee's supervisor called him in one day and told him the big boss had observed that he was coming in late much too often. I tell you, that'll help you wake up in the mornings!"

Finding more time

Most of us do not require as much sleep as we think we do. Just "a little sleep, a little slumber, a little folding of the hands," as we read in the Book of Proverbs. According to one writer, "if nine or ten hours are spent in bed every night, . . . about a third of the time is wasted—is not true sleep."[2] Another proven fact: the more you exercise, the less sleep you need.

Therefore, the first rule for "finding" more time is *get sufficient but not excessive rest*. Then *exercise*.

Check with your doctor if you have what you consider a real problem, such as the need for extra sleep, lack of endurance or lack of energy. Our bodies and our minds are so closely related that they catch each other's diseases.

Rule 2: Know your slump periods.

All of us have our energy peaks and slumps during the day. Use these times to best advantage. Don't save the odious tasks to do when you know you'll be wilted. Use your best hours for the most demanding of your day's work.

And remember that you and your mate may not have matching energy patterns. Virginia is a night person and Cy "dies to the world at eight o'clock." Cy is up and bouncing before Virginia opens her first eye in the morning. "Just as I'm getting ready to live—at about twelve noon—Cy is slowing down. He's great with Saturday morning chores, and I've been known to mop the kitchen floor at 2:00 A.M.!"

"I have a period," said Suzanne, "from about one to three o'clock in the afternoon when I literally wilt. But, after that, I catch up."

Rule 3: Stop dillydallying.

A friend said of her son-in-law and her daughter, "I know Leon is having a rough time with Peggy; she has always been so lackadaisical." Being lackadaisical at home where mother can recoup is one thing, but playing the same game with a husband—or wife—is something else.

Pick up your clothes as you go. Clear the table after meals. Clean messes as you make them.

During a discussion of adjusting to living together, Chad said their biggest problem was the ironing board, that it was *"always* in the kitchen doorway. Amanda invariably uses it, running five minutes late, and never has time to put it away." Nan, not believing what she had heard, asked, "What does she do with an ironing board?" We learned that Nan never irons, that she uses permanent press clothes which she takes from the dryer before they wrinkle. And Amanda irons her life away because "she stores her clothes on the closet floor, the bedroom floor, the bathroom floor."

Rule 4: Don't procrastinate.

There is a saying in the automobile industry that if a car is a lemon, it must have been made on Monday or Friday. You may have the Monday-Friday syndrome; you don't work well on Monday because you're just getting started, and you don't work well on Friday because you've run out of steam and you're anxious to quit. Or, putting it another way, you find it difficult to begin a job, easy to end it.

Dennis decides he's going to wash the car, then says there's no need, that it's probably going to rain. A week later, rain or shine, the car is still dirty.

It takes Jessica all evening to do dinner dishes for two. She may watch a TV show or walk the dog or finish her lesson plan, then two hours later look with dejection on the dirty dishes still waiting on the kitchen table. Then the slightest distraction will draw her from the kitchen again. All this for a chore that should consume twenty minutes. Troy calls their kitchen the "mess hall."

Rule 5: Don't lose things.

The hours we spend looking for the lost key or receipt

or book! Keep the key (or button or wallet) in your hand until you find the proper place to put it. File the receipt. Don't cover things—like books and shoes—with newspapers and sweaters.

Rule 6: Don't forget.
Make lists. Write notes to yourself. The dominant decor of my kitchen is the three-by-three note sheet: on the refrigerator "Thursday—7:30" (a party), on the cabinet door "cleaners" (*must* not forget the shirts), on the table "Beth and Barry" (call them after 6:00). As one efficiency expert says, "Do it now or write it down."

Keep a legal pad or notebook by your telephone. List your duties; check them off as they're completed. Compile the grocery list (daily) here. When you plan a trip, make a list of items to take, another of necessary chores. Find the largest calendar you can accommodate (a big area by your telephone is ideal!) and give your mind some help in remembering: social engagements, birthdays, holidays, the day your shoes will be ready at the repair shop, the weekend your cousin is coming to visit.

My friend Sarah had one such calendar. Every three months, for two consecutive Sundays, Alex serves on the money-counting committee at the church. So on her calendar, on these dates, Sarah had written "count money." A neighbor, seeing these entries, asked, "Wow! You and Alex set aside days to count your money?"

So, on your calendar, put "count money" if that's your way.

One of my most helpful records is my "guest and menus" book. In this, I put the date, names of my dinner (or breakfast or lunch or supper) guests and then the menu. If, a year later, the Smiths come for dinner again, I don't have to worry about giving them a repeat of the last meal. In this book I also make notations such as "Kenneth

doesn't like tuna"; "Wayne's favorite is pork chops";
"Bobbie is allergic to strawberries."

Buy a file cabinet.
Or use boxes. But file the papers you need to keep.
Newspaper clippings, magazine articles, ballet programs,
whatever. Cull its contents once a year—like the first
week in January. You will need a smaller file or metal lock
box for valuables such as voter's receipts, insurance
papers, automobile registrations, and medical records.
(We have in our metal box snapshots of our silver, crystal,
and china pieces so that for future emergency reference,
we'll be able to better estimate and substantiate any loss.)

At our neighborhood shopping center recently, I pulled
up beside a car from which houses could take a lesson.
Talk about being organized! In the middle of the front seat
was a partitioned box containing correspondence mate-
rials (pens, writing paper, envelopes, stamps, address
book), flashlight and batteries, road maps, first-aid kit
and medications, paperback books, and two whistles. On
the floor and seat of the back section, each in its place,
were umbrellas, boots, raincoats, sweaters, blankets,
pillows, and a radio.

Don't let the house gobble you up.
If things are completely out of hand and you dream of a
clean house, look for help. Put a notice on the high school
bulletin board requesting a one-day house-cleaner or
window-washer or grass-cutter. Or employ a teenage
neighbor. Wilma and three of her friends joined forces to
clean each other's houses, one each Saturday during the
months of April and October. "We get the works this
way: windows, floors, cabinets, everything."

If you choose to do your own household chores and
find the prospects overwhelming, break your work down

into manageable-size goals: this week, the bedroom; next week, the kitchen. One job completed gives you the stimulus to tackle the next one.

Avoid time-consumers.

Like TV. In our "Communication" discussions, we suggest choosing one night a week for keeping the TV turned off and using this night for talking to each other. Another benefit is the time you gain for whatever you'd like: talking, working, thinking, playing.

Carter said he realized one night that he had watched the evening news three times. So he eliminated two of his programs. Choose the TV shows you plan to watch, as you would select movies to see or books to read. Don't use the television set as a constant companion.

Just as pets cost money, they cost time. Care and feeding. Arrangements when you leave town. Trips to the veterinarian's.

Nathan and Rebecca's dog died after giving birth to puppies. For weeks, Nathan and Rebecca spent an hour and a half every morning and an hour and a half every evening feeding the puppies. "There really wasn't room in our schedule for those three hours." Even goldfish take time. "We never got around to cleaning the aquarium on time," said Harriett. "Finally we gave the aquarium, fish and all, to my nephew."

Then there is the story of the couple who took separate vacations because they didn't trust a third party to take care of their house plants!

For many young couples, the big time-consumer is getting to and from work, the hour or so a day on the freeways. Our classes suggested ways to make good use of this time:

Get in a car pool and make new friends.
Use a tape recorder and *talk* letters to your family.

Check out tapes from the library and listen as you drive to novels, short stories, plays, music, and political or business addresses.

Listen to radio news. Then you don't have to watch it on TV. Listen to nothing at all and enjoy the silence.

Memorize whatever you'd like to memorize: poetry, Scriptures, formulas, a speech you have to give, "what you're going to say to your wife when you get home."

"It seems to me that we spend half our lives going back and forth to the shopping center," said Randy. "I can name four nights last week that we had to go get something: milk one time, the next day a part for the kitchen faucet, gas in the car, etc." Planning ahead usually helps consolidate errands, gives you some additional hours at home, *and* saves gasoline.

Another suggestion: use what food you have on hand. There's a certain creative challenge in producing a meal even though the cupboard is bare—or almost. "At our house," said Eve, "every time we had company for dinner, Mother would send somebody to the store for something. Once I went to get *one* lemon! She'd call Daddy in from where he was visiting with our guests to whisper that she needed butter or tea or a loaf f bread. I vowed I'd never do that. So far, I haven't. It's rare that you can't find a substitute for what you need. Or do without."

Ginger complained to Boyd every time she did the wash because he put his undershirts in the laundry wrong side out. Then when she folded the clean clothes she had to turn the undershirts right side out. "I griped *every* time," said Ginger. "I kept asking 'Is it so much trouble to take them off right?' and he kept saying, 'Just leave them wrong side out; I don't mind turning them when I put them on.' So I did. It helped my disposition and made the job shorter. And Boyd really *doesn't* mind." Sometimes a little change makes a big difference.

I have a five-hour portable timer that, like Robert Louise Stevenson's shadow, goes in and out with me. It not only saves time, it saves face. It helps me remember a phone call I need to make or when I need to start dressing for an appointment. I set the timer to remind me to take the clothes out of the dryer or turn off the sprinkler or feed the dog. Sometimes I even use it for the cake in the oven.

Helping each other

Surely, in marriage, we can help each other in this business of making good use of our time. It should be obvious when help is needed, when frustration floats around.

In their book *Intimate Marriage*, the Clinebells write, "Certainly it is true that love and intimacy require *time* to grow. Middle-class adults are frantically over-scheduled. That this constant breathless running blocks out the occasions for closeness is undeniable. We live in a society in which it is easy to be too busy."[3]

"The time when I really want help," said Nell, "is when I'm rushing to get ready to go somewhere." Shirley's sentiments were in the same vein. "But," she added, "what really makes me angry is when Zack has me running ragged helping him find things. Then when he ends up dressed before I am, he yells at me for being late."

Donna likes help with the meals. Aaron appreciates the fact that Melissa writes letters to his folks when he's busy. Our question "When do you most often need and appreciate help?" brought these additional situations:

Washing the car. (From Dennis, of course!)
The last few minutes before a party at our house.
When I can't find something. ("Anna is a good looker!")

When I'm tired.
Or sick.
When I've made a mess of something. ("Like the cherry pie upside down on the kitchen floor!")
When I'm running late.
On Christmas Eve.
Early in the morning and late at night.
"The time I *don't* want help," said Dwight, "is when I'm packing the car."

Shirley Conran, in *Superwoman,* says, "Life is too short to stuff a mushroom."[4] But if stuffing mushrooms is your thing, the time is worth it. The choices are yours.

DISCUSSION STARTERS

1. When you were in school, when did you study for finals? (Discuss energy peaks.)

2. Is this time now your energy peak? If not, when are you most energetic? When does your slump come?

3. If a person is constantly late for appointments and dates, what does that say about his attitude toward people?

4. What items most frequently get lost at your house? Why?

5. What are your tricks for remembering things you need to do?

6. What type of filing system do you have?

7. List some time-consumers that you'd like to eliminate from your life.

8. When do you most often need and appreciate help from your spouse?

9. How do *you* find restoration from the daily routines of your life?

10. Discuss the case of Cy and Virginia. How does a couple with such diverse chemistry handle the need for working, living, and playing together?

10

FRIENDS

Our three preschoolers and I were sitting in the car waiting while Vernon said a lingering good-bye to his friend Bill. From the back seat, four-year-old Doug asked, "Are they cousins or something?"

What Doug was seeing was what Aristotle described as "a single soul inhabiting two bodies."

This closeness is our objective in choosing and keeping our friends. One of the few conclusions social scientists have reached about the chemistry of friendship is that it is a blending of similar pleasures and goals. A marriage without this relationship becomes stagnant.

Holly is congenial and outgoing; Grady is a private person. Holly grew up in a family surrounded by friends. *"Our* closest friends," said Grady, "were Aunt Lillian and Uncle Hubert." So developing friendships in the Holly-Grady marriage is a problem. However, Grady is working at being sociable—the first step in getting to know people. The relationship Holly wishes for Grady at this time is one normally experienced many years earlier. Experts tell us that a person robbed of certain important growing experiences in youth finds it more difficult to assume these roles later. The fact that Grady had missed the close friendship experience makes his current search for companionship an awkward one. But being married to Holly gives him the confidence and conviction he needs.

The search for new friendships is a phenomenon of our mobile age. Our parents and grandparents lived and died

113

on or near their own forty acres. But today young couples migrate to far cities to find or accept jobs for which they've trained. Once there, they begin new lives which need peer fellowship.

What friends can mean

To prepare for this book, questionnaires were mailed to former members of our groups. In response to the question, "Was the class beneficial to your marriage? If so, in what way?" the leading answer pertained to friendships. Samples:

> "Friendships we made have become a springboard for other things we've been able to do."
> "We've made what we consider lifelong friends, ones who support us and care for us, in spite of our moods and shortcomings."
> "Christian fellowship with Christian friends surely is an uplift!"
> "We learned so much about friends and friendships: that they lend perspective to your ups and downs, that deep fellowship is tempered with appreciation for the concerns of others, leading to even stronger friendships both within and between couples."
> "It's good to make friends, to know that other husbands leave socks on the floor too."
> "When we came, we knew no one in the group. Now our closest friends are people we met there. We spend a great deal of time together."

If you need to make friends, the time is *now*. It is more difficult as you grow older. In the middle years, most friendships are of long standing and it is difficult for newcomers to break in.

The *place* for making friendships is wherever you know you will find the kind of people with whom you want to relate: the church, the school, the office, the neighbor-hood.

We know that in order for a marriage to be vital and growing it must be involved with persons outside itself.

"Over-investment in a marriage," according to the Clinebells, "increases the mutual demand load" and puts a dangerous emotional burden on both husband and wife.[1]

What we expect from friendships

Have you noticed that most of the famous friendships are those involving *men?* David and Jonathan, John Alden and Miles Standish, Stanley and Livingston, Will Rogers and Wiley Post, Gayle Sayers and Brian Piccolo. Gener-ally, men develop stronger friendships than women do. Social research indicates several reasons.

Men have lower expectations of friendships. According to Dr. Sandra Candy, "Women are more apt to demand a deep level of trust and to terminate the relationship when they feel this has been violated."[2]

Intimacy is strong between female friends. They discuss the more private aspects of their lives, while a recent study among men shows that they seldom discuss per-sonal problems with their best friends.

Women make more demands on the time of their friends. They feel the need to keep in touch and even to be consulted about decisions and plans.

Lauren Bacall writes, "Bogie taught me something about friendship. He never pushed it—he demanded truth and loyalty, but he understood shortcomings, and accepted people more or less as they were. Whereas I wanted to know everything, be told everything—I made huge demands on my friends."[3]

Men are not as bothered with jealousy as women are. They do not deal in details as much as in generalities.

Yet we need to keep in mind, said one therapist, that men are more in the mainstream of society, spending their lives in the fellowship of men, whereas women, as a rule, have to reach out to develop relationships with other women.

Dr. Dobson suspects that cultural influences of early childhood "stamp a certain passivity on little girls, constricting their field of interests. For whatever reasons, the world of women is typically more narrow than that of men."[4]

But not Sadie's world. Sadie and Craig bowl together, play tennis and golf, and coach boys and girls. But it is on the women's basketball team that Sadie really shines! Craig cheers her on as she gets involved in tournaments in and out of the city. Their dream is to own a boat some day so that they can water ski together.

Somewhere in between Sadie and the wife on the sidelines we find the average young wife. Participation in activities together makes not only for good marriages, but for good friendships, with a variety of games to share.

The late psychologist Sidney Jourard pointed out that men are more apt to suffer from stress-related illnesses such as ulcers, hypertension and high blood pressure, in part "because they are less likely to use friendship as a therapeutic release."[5]

One of the most beautiful friendships I know is that of two women we met at M. D. Anderson Hospital in Houston. Texie Miklis has been a patient there for many months. Every week or so her friend Anna Dewberry comes from Dallas just to be with her. Texie can't talk because of surgical repairs to her face, but there is an affinity between her and Anna that is rare.

Jean and Candy are close friends. They and their husbands have made decisions to not have children. So, says Jean, with tongue in cheek, "since, according to statistics, Candy and I will be widows together, we have to take care of each other."

Being childless causes a unique strain on friendships, yet produces a stronger-than-usual alliance.

When friends intrude

There are times when friendships can be injurious to a marriage. Gretchen, for example, was beginning to wonder about the value of friends. "I've had it up to here with Wade's friends," she said. "They expect me to feed them, provide them a place for entertainment and, as often as not, a place to sleep." The problem had taken Gretchen and Wade to the office of a marriage counselor. Like many newlyweds, Wade had found no way to say to his friends, "Hey, I'm married now; I can't play anymore." Consequently, his bachelor buddies congregated at Wade and Gretchen's small apartment, usurping their privacy, ruining their good budget, and leaving belongings strewn about.

When Wade became aware of the impact of his friends' life style on his marriage and was given some tools for handling the situation, he took action. He and Gretchen agreed that once a week the boys would be invited over and be asked to contribute to the meal. Wade was able to explain that he and Gretchen were living on limited income and that married couples need time to themselves, that Gretchen liked to be with *her* friends too *and* that he and Gretchen needed to spend time with *couples*. As the counselor expected, the ties between Wade and his friends died a slow death when the friends followed other pursuits six nights a week and, eventually, found wives of their own.

Joy had a friend back home who, "on a dull week-end," would hop a bus and arrive, uninvited, at Joy and Peter's front door. "Peter was livid! And I wasn't much better." Finally, in much the same way that Wade had solved *his* problem, Joy explained the facts of married life to her friend and promised to "invite" her for a visit from time to time.

Who can be our friends?

Friends do not have to be in our age group. A. J. Gordon in "If I Were Twenty-One," wrote "I would have two or three choice friends among the older people." In a discussion of things we like to do, the lead question was, "If you had twenty-four hours to spend as you pleased, without your spouse, what would you do?" Owen's answer was poignant. "I'd go outside and sit under the tree with my friend Norman, who is seventy-six years old, and we'd talk. We'd probably talk mostly about cars, but he'd explain to me other things, like how to recognize an honest business deal and the value of a good wife and which cloud formations produce the thunderstorms. I'd stay there until time for him to go in to supper."

Max said, "Some of the people I work with are significantly older than I am, yet the problems we discuss are *very* similar."

Kitty spoke of a married couple with whom she and Wyatt spend a great deal of time. "Besides teaching us to play bridge, they're fun and we learn from them about life and about marriage and families."

Young people benefit from the knowledge and experience of older friends. The May-December relationship brings joy to both.

Much is written concerning the value to married persons of friends of the opposite sex. Experts in the field say that role expectations between the sexes is a major reason why such friendships are rare. However, they are more common among young people today than they were a generation ago. Caution is necessary, however, Dr. Candy says, since often women demand more intimacy than men are comfortable with. Men are likely to link emotional and sexual intimacy and therefore misinterpret friendly overtures.

Friendships between men and women often end when one of them gets married because one or both feel the marriage will suffer from the relationship.

The platonic friendship is more successful, we are told, in the middle years when fellowship grows out of professional experiences and when, according to a current poll, "the two have enough self-assurance to be less concerned about gossip."

Growing a friendship

How does one nurture a friendship? Hopefully, the growth is natural and mutually satisfying. But a full-blown friendship doesn't just happen. Someone asked, "Have you noticed that happy couples always know happy couples?" Maybe that's the big answer. No one wants to be pulled down or "used" in a friendship. We want to be made stronger by the friends we have. Your friends should make you better Christians.

June and Lester, Angela and Jeff were four marriage yearlings. For most of those twelve months they were always seen together. Then, suddenly, no regular foursome. June explained it this way: "We always felt that Angela and Jeff needed us. They had no family here and no close friends. So we started having them over and going out with them. But we almost never went to their place. And our conversations mostly concerned Angela's father's illness and Jeff's dissatisfaction with his job. We celebrated out first anniversary together by going out to a splurgy place and all. Then when Lester and I got home that night, we agreed that he and I need friendships too and that we don't receive from Angela and Jeff, we just give. So we're spreading ourselves around now and we're having fun and meeting some great people. And Angela and Jeff are still our friends."

The Clinebells say that one reason people fail to develop great friendships is because it takes up too much of their time. "We are too preoccupied with personal goals to invest the time and caring required. But clan relationships flourish only when there are interaction, communication and mutual need-satisfaction."

Friendship is described by one specialist as a "non-obligatory relationship between peers." But is it "non-obligatory?" Are we not indebted in friendships? Certainly we owe more than just fun. We owe stability, empathy, maturity, and joy.

Karen Burton Mains has written a book on the pleasures of sharing your home with others. "It really doesn't matter what size your rooms are," she says. "If hospitality is to begin anywhere, it must, like charity, begin at home."[6]

So begin in *your* home. Kyle and Jackie are always the first to offer their apartment for a meeting or a party, with never an apology for its smallness or its clutter. They often get out the sleeping bags and have guests spend the night rather than make a late drive home across town. People like being in their home; they like being their friends.

Jinnie gives gifts to her house guests. "It's to tell them 'Thank you for coming.'"

When Lil's car was in the shop for a week, Evan was able to let her use his car because their friend Fritz took him to work every day. Todd and Kelly were in the middle of painting the kitchen when they had to leave town suddenly. Duncan and Meg surprised them by going in and finishing the job.

Such acts of love nurture friendships.

"Why are your friends your friends?" we asked each other in our class.

"Because we're comfortable together."
"Because we think alike."
"Because they understand my folks."
"Because we laugh a lot."
"Because it's fun to be together even if we don't do anything special."
"Because she makes a great pecan pie!"
"Because when we're with them, I have a good feeling about the world."

But the true worth of friendship is not made manifest to the young. At age fifty you'll understand about tears and worry and pacing hospital floors and giving thanks and sharing joys and realizing how great it is to have a friend.

Recently we received from friends a note which said, "Our friendship through the years has made the dull times bearable and the good times *so* enjoyable!"

Don't lose time in developing friendships. As Gerald Moore entitled a recent article, "You Can't Do Without Other People."[7]

DISCUSSION STARTERS

1. How does childhood affect adult relationships?

2. In making new friends, how and where does one begin?

3. Is it more difficult to make friends as you grow older? Why?

4. Do a brainstorming of the names of pairs of famous friends. Why do you think most of them are men?

5. Who was your closest childhood friend? Are you still close friends? Why? Why not?

6. Discuss the advantages and disadvantages of platonic friendships between men and women; of friendships with older people.

7. If a husband says, "After all, I don't have to give up my friends just because I'm married," how should the wife respond? Use this idea as a format for role-playing.

8. Why are your friends your friends?

11

HAVING FUN

Hanging on our kitchen wall is a plaque which reads "Bloom Where You're Planted." Linda saw it and said, "Take it down fast, before Mike sees it!" Linda grew up in the mountains of Tennessee and she was having trouble adjusting to the mountains of New Mexico. "If Mike sees that," she said, "he'll have another slogan to throw at me."

In the years since then, Linda has learned to climb different mountains, to ski in the snow, to enjoy new friends, to keep busy with her growing family, and currently she is taking some college courses.

To bloom where you're planted means: "Make *the best* of your situation." Somehow *that* motto has always had a negative connotation, like: "You've got a bad deal, but learn to live with it." Actually "the best" is the ultimate; as an anonymous poet wrote, "To smother care in happiness and grief in laughter." Or, as another writer put it, "Lord, help me to keep my rejoicing current."

Fun means involvement

What is fun? How do you have fun? Dr. Mihaly Csikszentmihalyi writing in *Psychology Today*, describes fun as "flow." When we are involved in happy, rewarding activities, he says, "flow" emerges. We become

123

completely immersed in what we're doing and lose the sense of self and time. "A person gains a heightened awareness of his physical involvement and his enjoyment is enhanced."[1] This is what we call having fun.

So you must get involved. This does not mean you must perform, that you have to be the quarterback or that you are obligated to join the tennis club or take up skin diving. Stella is fantastic at playing the piano. It is one of our greatest pleasures to listen and watch. Cindy comes into our department every Sunday morning in a wheel chair; she is one of us and very involved. Harlan said he has a "fun wife." "What does she do?" "Oh, nothing special; she's just fun."

Keeping the fun in marriage

The sad commentary is that fun goes out of marriage much too often. The girl who, before marriage, enchanted her man with rippling laughter and high spirits loses this when she becomes a stern and solemn housewife. So does the personality kid who becomes a husband in solitary confinement.

"Before we were married," said Carla, "Lindsay would go anywhere with me, to the art shows, concerts, shopping even, and we had fun everywhere we went. Then we got married and he confessed that he didn't like museums and concerts and no longer felt obligated to go with me."

Walton said he laughed so much at work that he really liked to be "serious" when he got home!

Even though Lindsay may not have promised Carla out loud that he would go to art museums with her after marriage, his actions had left this inference. And no doubt the fact that Walton is basically a sociable person led his wife to expect more fun from him at home. To feel that you have been deceived is devastating. Bringing sensitive situations like these out in the open and discussing them can remove their sting and create an atmosphere for compromise.

So the scene changes. How to keep the drive alive? Obviously, a sense of humor helps. Humor does not mean being a great teller of jokes. "My introduction to the in-laws," said Jodie, "was nearly ruined when I tried to meet them with a joke and it went flat. I decided then and there to leave the funny stories to someone else and I'd do the laughing." Jodie has a marvelous one-liner sense of humor and she laughs a lot. As a young wife, I was often shocked going with my husband to plays and movies; he would laugh out loud before the punch line came! Our children tell us that the most fun they had at the adult parties in our home was "listening to Daddy and Mrs. Griffin laugh."

To have a *sense* of humor means just that, to *understand* it. To understand humor means participation and laughter. Dr. Joyce Brothers says that a good sense of humor makes one not only happier but also healthier. "Persons who lack a sense of humor are not as emotionally stable, nor are they as capable of enduring stress."[2]

Fun requires flexibility

Fun requires flexibility. Most newlyweds learn this right away. Mac liked surprises. So much so, said Maria, "that the big surprise was *no* surprise. He'd call and say, "Get dressed; we're going out," but he wouldn't say where. He'd move the furniture around. He slips extra money in her wallet. Once he came home from work at three in the afternoon just to surprise her. "When you're constantly geared for a surprise," said Maria, "you learn to be flexible."

Truman would welcome such flexibility in his marriage. He said, "You never ask Priscilla to go anywhere unless you give her a week's notice." Les is much the same. Once he is at home and out of his shoes, he doesn't budge from his chair. Les and Priscilla, as well as their mates, are missing out on some of the enjoyment of marriage.

Durward builds cars from odds and ends of automobile parts, with—we are convinced—toaster and radio pieces thrown in! For him this is fun. So Margaret has learned to live with the unfinished projects in the garage.

Some of the most routine aspects of marriage require the most adjustment. "For us it was getting a good night's sleep," said Carlton. "I snore; Susie has cold feet. She likes a warm room; I like it cold. She steals covers; I sleep diagonally. Neither of us wanted the alarm clock on our side of the bed. We laugh about it now, but, for a while, it wasn't funny."

Gloria Peron, 1978's "Queen of the Road," said she became a trucker because she was jealous of all of the "truck talk" from her husband and friends.[3] She acted on the maxim "If you can't lick 'em, join 'em." Maybe you need to pursue the same line. Not become a trucker, but "join 'em." Wives can watch TV football just as husbands can. Barry couldn't understand the fun of playing bridge until he learned the game. Ida agreed to go fishing with her husband "this one time"; now she can't get her fill. So if you haven't tried it, don't knock it.

Possibly there is no "good loser," but whatever your game, be a "tolerable" loser. Or winner. It is not uncommon to hear someone say, "I can't play with him. He's unbearable if he wins, or if he loses." Howard Finch of radio station KTRH in Houston quotes a poem which ends with these words: "If I should lose, let me stand by the road and cheer as the winners go by."[4]

Maria's husband Mac, with his love of surprises, wasn't

completely off base. Surprises, pleasant surprises, help to keep the fun in marriage.

Barbara Chafin was talking to a group of women one morning, and, from time to time as she looked at her notes, she saw other notes that her husband had added. Like "Right on!" and "Very good!" Another time he put a blue ribbon on the refrigerator to signify that her meal was a winner.

Dan Yeary, when he served as Single Adult Minister at our church, told of having lunch with a group of associates, among them a newlywed husband who had *his* lunch in a paper bag. From out of the bag he pulled love notes and drawings that carried private messages. "We laughed and gave him a hard time," said Dan, "but actually we were envious."

Ford writes notes in Rosemary's recipe books. "Add more liquid" or "Wow!" and, once, "Yours is better than Annie's." Rosemary puts love notes in his suitcase, along with an occasional sack of homemade cookies or a new book. She found an old love letter he had written to her, put it in an envelope, and mailed it to his office.

Rex said he had been married almost three years when one day as he passed a flower shop, he remembered how he used to send Ida flowers and buy her gifts on his lunch hour. "I realized how long it had been since I had done anything that wasn't completely expected or anything foolish, like I used to do."

"I think," said Ida, "that was the day he came home with the rubber chocolates!"

Fun and foolishness

There are times when a marriage needs something that's utterly foolish, when caution is thrown to the wind and the routine is broken.

One Saturday morning Irving and Caroline set out in their car to go they didn't know where. "We just decided to drive until we found a place where we'd like to spend the day and night. It was great fun. We're ready to do it again. This time with another couple maybe. It was the first time in my life," said Caroline, "that I had ever been *anywhere* without knowing exactly where I was going."

Eddie and Melba decided they'd go to bed early, turn out the lights, and listen to the radio mystery program. It was such fun that they still do it often.

Two husbands kept a devious battle of water guns with each other alive for months.

So go to an auction. Have breakfast in bed. Work up a touch football game. Bake a cake with a surprise in the middle. As the saying goes in the profession of interior designers, "There's charm in the unexpected."

Remember dating?

Marriage counselors suggest that couples periodically go dating. One counselor said, "Start from the very beginning. Call her for a date, just like you used to. Pick her up, hold the car door open, do it the way you did it when you were single. Go to a special place and try to impress each other."

Steve Berman, writing in the magazine *New Marriages*, tells of one such date he and his wife Vivien Weiss have each year. "Every year we re-enact our first meeting. We put on the same clothes and go to that same spot on the same date—ten minutes to 2:00. She comes up and asks me directions to Merrill Hall. I don't know, so I turn to ask someone else. We go through all the things we did that day and say the same things. . . . I'm looking forward to our 50th meeting."[5]

Rick and Juanita have a similar memory trip they take. They like to go back to their college campus on a school day, walk with the students going to classes, sit on the familiar benches, and eat in the dining hall where they first saw each other.

Vacations can be fun

Vacations, intended to be happy times, are often disasters. It's hard to spend that much money and still be cheerful. Or *he* wants to go camping and *she* wants to stay in a motel. Sometimes there's a two-way pull from parents vying for visits.

As a rule, vacations are scheduled, so they should not come as a surprise. Start planning months ahead. Planning is half the fun. Gather brochures and maps. Read them together. Go to the library and check out books on the places you plan to see. Check your newspapers for travel articles and for times and locations of travel movies.

Make a list, long in advance, of the items to pack. Be sure to include necessary addresses and phone numbers, film for your camera, and if you're going by car, emergency articles such as first-aid kit, flashlight, blankets, umbrellas, all your maps and brochures and everything that goes in your suitcase. Remember the motto "Take twice as much money as you think you'll need and half as much clothing." If you like to read to each other as you travel (yes, some people do), take along a book of short stories or magazines or travelogues—no "to be continued" types. Remember your favorite pillows and *an extra set of keys* (plus a third set in a magnetic box under the chassis).

Start putting away the necessary money, whether it's a small amount or half a month's salary. Decide what you'll do, where you'll go. If you're going to visit family, try to find some side trips to take en route. One summer Flo and Preston decided to go with friends to Colorado rather than to make the usual trips to visit their parents. So a month before, they took one day off from work and Flo had a long week-end with her parents while Preston visited his family.

Philip likes to go camping. Bess detests the dust and insects and dirty clothes, cooking and eating outside, cleaning up—everything about it. So for the past two summers they've hit upon a compromise. They and another couple have bought camping gear together. The husbands and wives have agreed that for every two nights of camping they will spend one night in a motel. This is an equal division of money ("if you don't count the cost of the camping equipment") and the wives "get to have a real bath" every third night.

Whenever your vacation time comes and for whatever length it is, plan to get away from home at least for two or three days. Our minds and bodies need periodic re-creation.

Celebrate!

A party is premeditated fun. The main ingredient of a party is people. Everything else—food, place, clothes, entertainment—is secondary. The popular hosts are those who make their guests feel comfortable.

If you are having trouble deciding to have a party, get invitations (or make them), and mail them. Once you've committed yourself, you're forced into action.

Start with an idea or a reason. Or give a party for no reason at all. Weldon never knows his weekend schedule until quitting time on Friday. So he and Regina give many spur-of-the-moment parties. What they like best to do is invite three other couples over for cards and pizzas.

Celebrate anything. Like the coming of spring. Election day, daylight saving time, graduations, promotions, retirements; to announce a pregnancy, to welcome a new friend to the city, to use your empty living room. Have a box supper or a quilting bee. Make homemade ice cream. Have a picnic in your own backyard—or patio or porch or driveway.

One family had a progressive dinner all in their own house: appetizer in the living room, salad in the kitchen, main course in the dining room, and dessert on the patio. We had a January birthday party at our house, placing guests at four different tables, determined by the season of the year in which they were born. Each group had menus and table settings typical of the seasons. Once I took the fourteen school lunch pails down from the pantry shelf and filled them for a high school graduation luncheon. One of the happiest parties we had was the time we had a tremendous amount of food left over from a Saturday brunch. So, in Pied Piper fashion, we went down the street inviting neighbors in for lunch.

And store this idea away for your thirty-three-and-a-third year anniversary! Paul and Mary, Vernon and I married two weeks apart, so we have often celebrated anniversaries together. This year was special. Paul and Vernon surprised their wives with a third-of-a-century anniversary party!

You may not have a guest room or extra sleeping space at your house, but, with whatever arrangements you can make, try to have friends and relatives in for overnight or weekends. These occasions will provide some of your happiest times.

Eating for fun

It is as true now as when it was first said that "the way to a man's heart is through his stomach." Variations on the theme, such as "When do we eat?" or "Is it for dinner or just dessert?" attest to the importance of food in our lives. That doesn't mean we should be slaves to cooking and serving and cleaning. Having people in for a meal *can* be easy.

Karen Mains, in her book, lists her shortcuts for entertaining:

1. Never clean before company.
2. Don't be afraid to do things with a flair. ("An old patchwork quilt for a table cloth, huge baskets of dried fall weeds.")
3. Do as much ahead of time as possible.
4. Clean as you go.
5. Use all the help that comes your way.[6]

Your meals do not have to be six-course ones. Try spaghetti and a salad, make-your-own pizza or omelet, a good soup or chowder or chili in the winter, cold chicken salad and fruit in the summer, hamburgers that the men cook while the women toss a salad. Or vice versa.

If you really want to do it up big, don't save it all to do that day. Be in control when your guests arrive. Try to allow for a thirty-minute breather or a long bath before you start the last-minute jobs. Be relaxed and your guests will be relaxed. Don't rush through the meal; keep the conversation humming. Consider a dessert that can be served from its container; bring the custard to the dining table in a large crystal bowl or the cake on a cake stand.

Most Americans eat more food than they need, so try cutting back—to keep your weight as well as your food bill in check. Rich likes macaroni and cheese, but he considers it a side dish; to Eleanor it is the main course. Patsy knows Leonard likes sundaes, so she serves them almost daily. "We've had a month of sundaes," he punned. Bill Wylie says that the amount of food his mother would put in his lunch box was determined by how hungry she was when she packed his lunch.

For many couples, the daily menu is tinged with

emotion. "Sometimes," said Heidi, "I think food is the most important thing in Virgil's life." Morley strongly resented the "short course in nutrition" that Myra was giving him instead of serving "just plain food that I like." Meal times (and school lunches, snacks, party foods) have nostalgic associations for most of us. We turn loose slowly.

Use all those wedding gifts to enhance your table. Use your silver and china. Put place mats on the table. Use as many different vases and bowls and figurines as you have, for centerpieces. Create an idea or a color. Use candles and flowers and greenery. Put a basket of fruit or vegetables in the center of the table.

Make meals special for just the two of you. Buy two cheap place settings for the fun of something new. (I have noticed that when Jon, our bachelor son, comes over and cooks for himself, he uses the *pretty* dishes, the ones in the other cabinet.) And sit at the table to eat. No TV, no newspaper.

Ira had taken Florence out to eat on Friday night at a new French restaurant. It was such a special evening that Florence decided to transfer the idea to her own house. So the next Friday evening, Ira said, she "really laid it on me!" She duplicated the menu, the centerpiece (with candlelight), the music, even the tablecloth.

A friend tells of her experience with her recent attempt at having an intimate dinner for two. The last child had left home to go to college, so, on a Friday night, the mother decided to have her romantic dinner. She set up a small table in the living room with candles and flowers, and pheasant-under-glass. And, just as she and her husband sat down at the table, in walked the unexpected daughter home for the week-end. She looked at her parents with an "at your age!" embarrassment and went on upstairs!

Every Thursday Spencer has lunch with friends, each taking turns at choosing the place to eat. Recently, when it was Spencer's day of choice, Jeannie packed lunches and the four business men brown-bagged it!

Eating isn't just for staying alive; eating is for fun. "A feast is made for laughter" (Eccles. 10:1).

The fun of working

The happy times don't have to be just the times when we play and eat. Work can be fun too. Hugh and Brenda are do-it-yourself-ers. They have built much of the furniture in their house and have refinished old pieces. Guy and Anita work together in the yard. Your attitudes determine whether it's fun to wash the car together, cook, clean, shop, do the laundry, or whatever needs to be done around your house.

There is happiness to be found beyond the limits of your home and the circle of your friends. Try reaching out to the children and adults around you who need special kinds of help: the patients in the hospital, the men and women in the retirement homes, children at the day care center. Get involved at your church. Help with the Boy Scouts or the cancer drive. Become friends with a foreign student. There is fun akin to love in "doing it unto one of the least of these."

The fun in marriage is not always in *doing*; it is in *being*. Being married to each other, being in love, being young, being healthy. But work is necessary to *keep* the marriage fun. So brighten the corner where you are; bloom where you're planted.

DISCUSSION STARTERS

1. What do you like to do for fun? Alone? With a group?

2. What would you say is the main reason that fun goes out of so many marriages?

3. Get as many definitions as possible for "a sense of humor."

4. Discuss the advantages and disadvantages of surprises in marriage.

5. On cards, ask each person to list his/her five favorite ways to have fun. Let couples compare answers.

6. What is your favorite vacation trip from your childhood? Why? Imagine—or pretend—that your spouse was with you on that occasion. Would he/she have enjoyed it as much as you did? Why? Why not?

7. What was the most unique party you ever attended?

8. When was the last time you laughed "till your sides hurt"? Why?

9. Do you think most TV shows are geared to men's likes?

10. Make a copy of each of the following situations. Give one to a wife, one to a husband for role playing:
    HUSBAND: You start the conversation by telling

your wife that it was announced at the office today that vacation times must be reserved this week. Therefore you and she need to decide on a time and make plans.

Present these ideas to her: If you go on your vacation before July 4, you can use Jim's camper. You'd like to go camping in the Ozarks sometime in June. Camping is an inexpensive type vacation (especially when you can borrow a camper). You relax better outdoors. You like getting away from the city. Fresh air is healthy. You can park the camper and avoid traveling during bad weather. You do not have to make reservations or fight the tourist traps.

Add any other ideas you like.

WIFE: Your husband announces he wants to use a friend's camper so that the two of you can go on an outdoor vacation trip. You do not like camping out.

Present these ideas to him: You'd rather have three days in motels with no cooking than a week of housekeeping at some camp. You don't like the outdoors. Or insects. Or bad weather (wet, hot, or cold). It's no vacation if you do not have a good bathroom.

Add any other ideas you'd like to use.

11. What makes you happy?

12

FAMILY RITUALS

"November first is our panic day," said Shelley. "That's when we realize Thanksgiving and Christmas are coming and we have a lot of problems ahead of us."

To borrow from Dickens, the holidays can be "the best of times and the worst of times." For many young couples it's hard to see the "best" because of the "worst." The problem of how to share the holidays with two sets of in-laws brings gloom and dread inside many apartments. Not to mention the arguments. Shelley and Edward still hadn't settled the dilemma of sharing families, so the approaching holidays were grim times for them. No single subject in our group discussions was so charged with apprehension as was that of where to spend Thanksgiving and Christmas.

The most common solution is to alternate visits: this year, Thanksgiving with her folks, Christmas with his; next year, the reverse.

Shelley and Edward had decided to do it like this, but somewhere along the way there was a breakdown in communications between them and their families. Since Shelley and Edward live in the same city as Shelley's parents, it was decided that the first Christmas would be spent with Edward's folks, Thanksgiving with Shelley's. The next year they went to the distant city to be with Edward's parents for Thanksgiving—planning, of course, to be with the other in-laws at Christmas. But two weeks before Christmas, Edward began to get pleas from his mother to be with them for the holidays. "I am the baby of the family," said Edward, "and all my brothers and sisters were going to be home for Christmas. My mother could not bear the thought of the broken circle. So I went home, I really did! And left Shelley to spend Christmas with her family. I was gone less than two days, but it was a miserable Christmas."

"The problem isn't with us," said Shelley, "it's with parents. Not just ours, but with so many others I know."

Many parents, like Edward's, feel that their out-of-town child should be with them on holidays if he or she happens to live in the town with in-laws. "And that's not fair," said Grace. "I'd hate to think I'd never get to spend Christmas with my parents just because I happen to live in the same town with them."

On the Sunday before Christmas, Lorraine was having a *very* difficult time. Blake had only two days off for Christmas. Lorraine is an only child. Her mother lives six hundred miles away. Lorraine and Blake had invited her to be with them for Christmas, explaining that there was not enough time to travel to her place nor enough money to fly. Responses from Lorraine's mother were upsetting. She said she could not leave her invalid father and that he was unable to travel. "She keeps begging us to come and I keep saying, 'We can't; there's no way.'"

As Lorraine and Blake discussed their problems, I observed, sitting across from them, a misty-eyed Jana.

The Sunday after Christmas everyone was anxious to know about Lorraine and Blake's Christmas. "I could hardly enjoy ours for worrying about yours," said Jana. "Well, we stayed at home," said Blake. "Lorraine's mother found someone to take care of Lorraine's grandfather, so that she could spend three days with us."

"Next year we'll know to get worried sooner," said Lorraine.

Averting the family tug-of-war

Such tugs-of-war are hard on marriages. They should not be allowed to happen. We have accumulated some answers for you; we hope they help.

First, of course, *talk about it*. Early. Don't get painted into a corner. Before the panic day arrives, discuss your ideas *and* make a decision. In making that decision, there are several things to keep in mind. One is: don't be unbending; bring your families in on your thinking. If you are going to begin an alternating visit program, let them help you decide where to begin. If you have married brothers and sisters, get with them and work out coinciding schedules.

When your plans are finalized, *be sure they are clear to both sides of the family*. Discuss them lovingly.

Be subject to change. One Christmas Trudy's mother was quite ill; it was important to be with her father and brother. "Last year we were supposed to spend Thanksgiving with my folks," said Joanne, "and we decided to go skiing. I'm sure they were disappointed, but they were glad we had the good deal on the skiing trip."

Remember that Christmas and Thanksgiving are special times and *it's difficult for your parents to be separated from you*. "Probably they feel the same way about being away from *us*," said Stephanie, "as we (husbands and wives) would about being away from each other."

Consider inviting them to your house. Both families or one each year.

Doctors Henry Jordan and Leonard Levitz, in *Bon Appetit*, go along with this. "Your parents have invited you to a holiday dinner, and so have your in-laws. Do you go to one house for a big midday feast and a few hours later sit down for dinner at the other? That's one way, but wouldn't it be better if you could agree to celebrate with each set of parents on an alternate year? Better yet, invite both sides of the family to your house."[1]

A "Dear Abby" reader wrote, "Please urge young marrieds to dare to have their own holiday celebrations in their own homes. Suggest that they invite their parents and grandparents, who might even be relieved to be finally free of the burden of entertaining three generations."

Remind yourself that it really is important to be with family for these special times. "I can attest to that," said Henry. "The first Christmas after we were married we tried to juggle visits to both families, and that had its problems. So the next year, since we had moved across the country, we decided we'd be big and brave and stay at our house for Christmas. Just the two of us. Paige kept saying, 'I just can't get the Christmas spirit,' and, on Christmas Day, she cried buckets. I felt the same way she did, but I couldn't see *both* of us sobbing all day!"

"I know," said Joanne. "When we went skiing at Thanksgiving, it just didn't seem like Thanksgiving."

Don't wear yourself out the week before Christmas. Situations seem twice as bad and emotions are twice as vulnerable when you're upset because time is running out. Plan ahead. Shop and cook early. (One father we know does not allow anyone in the family to purchase Christmas gifts *after Thanksgiving!* That may be drastic, but his family does get the Christmas shopping done early.)

Thanksgiving made easy

Now that you've exercised your options and made your plans, you have work to do. You are coming upon the most enchanting time of the year and you want it to be beautiful—and you want it to enrich your marriage. Thanksgiving is not as big as Christmas, but it is a family time.

A friend recently told of her most memorable Thanksgiving. "It was just last year. We have a new daughter-in-law. Before I got around to making plans, she called and invited us to their place for Thanksgiving dinner. She also invited her own parents, who live here also. I asked if I could bring something and, without fanfare, she suggested I bring a mincemeat pie. When the day came, my husband and I slept late, read the paper, had the first relaxed Thanksgiving of our married lives. When we arrived at our son and daughter-in-law's house, they were having coffee, completely at ease. Half an hour later, we sat down at the table, which was set with paper plates and paper cups, to a meal of smoked turkey (which our son had done outside), baked sweet potatoes (still whole), green beans, my mincemeat pie, and her mother's congealed salad. When we finished eating, we spent fifteen minutes cleaning the kitchen and two hours visiting! I didn't know Thanksgiving could be so pleasant!"

If you can make *your* guests feel this good, you will have given them one more thing for which to be thankful. If you are helping your folks or your in-laws at their house, exert what influence you can for simplicity. You don't *have* to use paper plates or limit your menu. But planning and working ahead can make for a more restful day.

Our class discussed Thanksgiving memories. Among them were these:

"The time, when I was nine or ten, and my granddad and I picked up pecans in the back yard."
"The year we visited my Aunt Ella and she gave us a big box of Christmas gifts to take home with us. All the way home I

kept wondering what was in those packages and just knowing I couldn't wait 'til Christmas."

"The time Mom used the construction paper turkey I'd made at school for the centerpiece on our Thanksgiving table."

"The time—I was about four—we went around the table and told what we were thankful for—and they didn't skip me."

So Thanksgiving is for building memories too. And giving thanks.

The best gifts give you

One of my recollections of Christmas is watching my father wrap the packages for mailing—how his fingers manipulated the twine, crossing and rewinding it and tying it together at all the places where it crossed. (And now the post office doesn't want us to use twine because it fouls up the mechanisms!)

Gifts are a very real part of Christmas. They come in all categories: tangible and intangible, large and small, expensive and inexpensive, self-made and purchased, romantic, nostaligic, funny.

Beth went to school one summer and learned to home-can the vegetables she and Barry were raising in the garden. For Christmas gifts, they give beautiful jars of beans, peas, corn, and tomatoes. Beth creates gifts of découpage, ceramic and china painting, and wall hangings. Barry has given hammocks of his own making.

Frank and Jeanette give gifts from Frank's workshop. Mary gives a variety of presents of her own creation. Joye makes gifts on her sewing machine or with her knitting needles. Lois puts homemade goodies in unique containers. Mildred bakes breads and cookies and ties them up in cellophane and ribbons. Gene gives snapshots from his own camera. Joan does embroidery and crewel. Drifty writes songs. Mary Lee makes chocolates and mints from her molds. Peg bakes and decorates cakes. Vivian makes scrapbooks. Pop gives his home-grown plants. Reese and Sherry make candles. Bill does macramé.

In spite of our suggestions that she cut down her list, my mother buys and wraps fifty-five (current count) Christmas gifts each year for the three generations of her family. One year Muggy wrapped all her presents in newspapers, tied them with red yarn and wrote messages on them with a red felt pen. Smashing! Nell makes handsome gift containers by covering old boxes. One family draws names and each person makes and fills a stocking for his recipient.

From one family we receive a puzzle every year, from another a candle. Jean buys Christmas gifts all twelve months as she travels with her husband. George sends fruitcakes from a favorite small town bakery. Mike and Linda buy handmade gifts from the New Mexico Indians.

When we ask about most cherished or most memorable Christmas gifts, almost always they are gifts insignificant in monetary value. Like "the earring I thought I had lost," or "a ribbon to tie around my finger to remind me of her love." ("And he wore it too—'til Christmas Day was over.") "She put some patches in a box, which I knew meant she *would* patch those old Levis that she really wished I'd throw away." Vivian wrapped a tiny baby doll and gave it to Mother in lieu of the grandchild due to arrive in August.

Trees and trimmings

Don't feel that you have to buy a complete outlay of tree ornaments and lights your very first Christmas. It's fun to add to them each year. Beth and Barry's first tree was decorated with only the white doves and bells from the wrappings on their wedding gifts. Don and Stella picked up pine cones and sweet gum balls in the woods and used them to decorate their first tree. One family puts only edibles on their tree; these they give to those who visit them during the holidays. For each of her four Christmases, Laura has received a bear ornament from her great Uncle Vernon. At this rate, by the time she gets married, she should be able to adequately trim a tree with bears.

It is fun to count off the days as Christmas approaches, such as with an Advent calendar. One family marks the days with what they call a "journey." They put the figures of Mary, Joseph, and the Baby Jesus in a home-made manger under the Christmas tree. On the dining room table they place the Three Wise Men. A week before Christmas, the Wise Men begin their journey to Beth-lehem, being moved an equal number of feet each day.

At our house, the *years* were marked with a nativity scene. The first year we bought the manger, Jesus the next year, Mary the following year—until now, sixteen years and sixteen carved wooden figures later, we have a completed set.

The Christmas meal should be as festive as it is bountiful. Bring out the good china and the red table cloth and an array of candles. Serve with a flair, you in your hostess dress and your husband wearing his red bow tie. Your meal may come on Christmas Eve or Christmas Day. Bill and Susan have a Mexican Christmas Dinner on December 24 for just friends. The next day they eat with relatives. Teresa said her family always invited for dinner one person or one family "that we did not know last year." Sometimes it would be new friends. Another time it might be a person from out of town who had a family member in a local hospital. Once it was a college student who couldn't get home because of bad weather. Perry's parents work with homeless boys, so "we always had four or five extra boys at Christmas."

"Mother never liked Christmas leftovers," said Jan, "so

after dinner, she would have all of these little packages and containers of desserts and turkey and bread that she would give to our guests as they left."

Building your own Christmas traditions

When two people marry, they usually bring together strong family traditions. There are numerous compromises to be made, especially when these traditions pertain to Christmas. Perhaps you discussed them before you married. If not, get on with it. When to put up the tree—Christmas Eve or two weeks before? What kind of tree—a real one or should you invest in an artificial one? When will you open the presents—Christmas morning or the night before? How about stockings? Will you send out Christmas cards? How many? What kind? We save the Christmas cards we receive each year, put them in the red basket in the kitchen and through the year we take out one a day and hang it (with a laundry hook hanger—such as fits over the shower rod) on the kitchen cabinet door (along with the 3" × 3" note sheets!). The name on the card is our person or family to pray for and think about that day.

To enjoy the Christmas season, get involved. Have a tree-trimming party. Go caroling. Wrap presents together. (Many husbands like wrapping packages.) Attend a Christmas concert. Get the tedious things out of the way—like shopping, addressing cards, baking—so that you can get caught up in the spirit of love and giving. Merry Christmas!

Other holidays

Easter can have its traditions too: dyeing eggs, putting a filled basket in the center of the table, dressing up for church, going to the park. Trent and Celia had an adult

Easter egg hunt. New Year's Eve and New Year's Day are good days for getting together with friends. Nancy and Larry have had a December 31 buffet for their friends since the first year they were married. Valentine's Day can be special for just the two of you—whatever is romantic. A heart-shaped cake, handmade valentines, original poetry, dinner out. Look ahead to July 4, Halloween, and other holidays as times to do something special for each other or for others.

Birthdays

Most family traditions are associated with holidays, but for some families, birthdays are times of great celebration. In Chuck's home, on the day that you had a birthday, you were the "cock of the rock." From the time you woke up in the morning until you fell asleep at night, it was *your* day! The family showered the honored member with gifts and parties, the mother produced a birthday cake made to order, and all the cards and gifts that came in the mail were saved for the big hour. Everyone sang "Happy Birthday" and you felt very special. With this as a background, Chuck told about his first birthday after he and Natalie married.

"I just knew she was planning a big surprise party for me. All day at work I kept thinking 'When I get home, I'll walk in the door and there'll stand all my friends ready to sing "Happy Birthday."' I could just see the streamers on the ceiling and the balloons and the big cake with candles and decorations. Well, I went home, walked in the door and there was no one there but Natalie. I said to myself, 'Well, this is just to throw me off; they'll be coming later.' So I sat down in my chair and tried to act nonchalant. I was sure the puttering Natalie was doing in the kitchen was frantic last-minute party preparation and I didn't want to spoil it by peeking.

"A few minutes later she called me to dinner. Even while I was sitting at the table, I kept expecting some kind of big surprise. We finished. She had baked a cake and she gave me a book she knew I wanted. That was it! No balloons, no people darting out from under the bed! Even when we were ready to go to sleep that night, I kept thinking, 'They're still gonna come!'"

Natalie did not grow up with all the birthday revelry. To her way of celebrating, the day had been duly marked.

One of my most memorable birthdays was the year we were vacationing at a cabin in the Colorado mountains, many miles from the nearest town. Jinnie and Dana put on a most adequate party with a cake baked in an inadequate oven, gifts wrapped in grocery sacks and tied with string—and a centerpiece of wildflowers!

On one of Vernon's birthdays, the children and I gathered all the unused gifts he had received for many Christmases and birthdays and Father's Days and rewrapped them as his presents from us.

Just for family

There will be some family rituals from both of your families you will want to keep, some you will want to discard, and some that will begin with you. All will enrich your marriage. Like these:

French toast on Saturday mornings (at our house).
A family reunion periodically. (We have one every other summer, the next brother or sister agewise choosing the spot, making the arrangements, and being in charge.)
Ribbons on doors or mail boxes to signify something special (like the blue one on Phil and Jeanne's mailbox when Fletcher was born).
Bringing out the wedding album on anniversaries. (Harry and Jinnie have done this for thirty-three years.)
Having homemade ice cream on the first day of summer.

And watermelon on July 4.
Denoting the seasons, as Betty does, with appropriate front door decorations.

Thomas sort of put it all together for us when he said, "I hadn't thought much about rituals before now; we didn't have much tradition at our house. But I think traditions are valuable because we all need something in our lives to give continuity, to keep us linked to the past *and* the future, to make us feel that we're a part of the scheme of things."

DISCUSSION STARTERS

1. If you and your spouse had to spend Thanksgiving alone, how would you observe the day?

2. Have you solved the problem of where to spend your Christmases? Share it with us.

3. If you looked at Christmas from your parents' perspective, would you have a different feeling about Christmas?

4. Why is Christmas such a hassle for most of us? What can be done to avoid the panic?

5. Do you spend more money for Christmas presents than you do for all other gifts throughout the year? Why? Why not?

6. What is your most memorable Thanksgiving? Christmas?

7. What is the most unique Christmas gift you ever received? The most cherished?

8. If you could keep only one Christmas tradition, what would it be?

9. Were you ever away from home at Christmas? What were your thoughts?

10. How were birthdays celebrated in your family? Do you plan to continue these ideas?

11. Have a brainstorming of family traditions and rituals that group members know of or have been a part of.

12. Are traditions just a natural part of our lives (could we really avoid them?) or do they require reinforcement?

13. In what way are family rituals valuable?

My brother Harry didn't get to see my book. He died November 24, 1980.

I was an enchanted college student the morning I sat and listened to this tall, handsome, poetry-quoting, science-loving brother deliver the Youth Sunday sermon, which he had entitled *Life Is a Poem*. He emphasized the fact that poets, like other people of greatness, often suffer for their art. So did he. For twelve years he endured pain so that we might have the joy of his presence.

His friend Robert Browning wrote it, but Harry lived it:

> Ah, but a man's reach should exceed his grasp,
> Or what's a heaven for?

NOTES

Chapter 1

1. Lance Morrow, "Wondering if Children are Necessary," *Time*, 5 March 1979, pp. 42–47.

2. John Drakeford, *The Home: Laboratory of Life* (Nashville, TN: Broadman, 1965), p. 5.

3. Kahlil Gibran, *The Prophet* (New York: Alfred A. Knopf, 1923), p. 20.

4. Dr. James Bossard and Dr. Eleanor Bell, *The Girl That You Marry* (Turbatville, PA: Macrae Smith Co., 1960).

Chapter 2

1. Dr. James Dobson, *What Wives Wish Their Husbands Knew About Women* (Wheaton, IL: Tyndale House Publishers, 1975), p. 114.

2. Gail Sheehy, *Passages* (New York: E. P. Dutton, 1976), p. 95.

Chapter 3

1. Ray Short, "Cupid's Many Slings and Arrows," UPI, *Houston Post*, 14 February 1979.

2. Dr. Joyce Brothers *Houston Post*, 27 April 1978.

3. Dr. Jesse Potter, *Iowa Spectator*, March 1978, p. 8.

4. Dr. Arthur C. Wassmer, *Making Contact* (New York: Dial Press, 1978, p. 190.

5. Liz Smith, *The Mother Book* (Garden City, NY: Doubleday and Company, 1978), p. 292.

6. Dr. Anthony Pietropinto and Jacqueline Simenauer, *Beyond the Male Myth* (New York: Times Books, 1977).

7. Jack Smith, *Spend All Your Kisses, Mr. Smith* (New York: McGraw-Hill Co., 1978), p. 28.

Chapter 4

1. Dr. Albert Ellis, New York Institute for Rational Living.

Chapter 5

1. Dr. Walter Toman, in *Washington Post*, 1975.

2. Marian Martin, "It's Just Not Natural," *Home Life*, July 1974, p. 30.

3. Reuben Herring, *Building A Better Marriage* (Nashville, TN: Convention Press, 1975), p. 41.

4. Dr. Maurice Prout, "How Not to Feel Guilty," *Houston Post*, December 1978.

5. Georgie Galbraith, "Lines to a Daughter-in-Law," used by permission of Gail Kirkman.

6. Jane Howard, *Families* (New York: Simon and Schuster, 1978), p. 17.

Chapter 6
1. Ralph Waldo Emerson, "Love" from *Essays of Emerson* (New York: A. L. Burt Co.), p. 122.

Chapter 7
1. John Drakeford, *The Home: Laboratory of Life* (Nashville, TN: Broadman, 1965), pp. 66–69.

2. Ogden Nash, "A Word to Husbands," in *I Wouldn't Have Missed It* (Boston: Little, Brown and Co., 1972), p. 334.

3. Dr. Joyce Brothers, *Houston Post*.

4. Mobil Corporation, *Saturday Review*, 14 April 1979, p. 23.

Chapter 8
1. Dr. David Mace, *What Makes a Marriage Happy?* (New York: Public Affairs Pamphlets, 1959), no. 290, p. 11.

2. Howard Hovde, *The Neo-Married* (Valley Forge, PA: Judson Press, 1968), p. 38.

3. John D. Bloskas, *Staying in the Black Financially* (Nashville, TN: Convention Press, 1977), p. 20.

4. Reuben Herring, *Building A Better Marriage* (Nashville, TN: Convention Press, 1975), p. 38.

5. Dr. James Dobson, *What Wives Wish Their Husbands Knew About Women* (Wheaton, IL: Tyndale House Publishers, 1975), p. 105.

Chapter 9
1. Dr. Tom Bourne, Bourne and Potts Marriage and Family Consultants, Houston, TX.

2. *Current Literature,* May 1912, pp. 549–50.
3. Howard and Charlotte Clinebell, *The Intimate Marriage* (New York: Harper and Row, 1970), p. 49.
4. Shirley Conran, *Superwoman* (New York: Crown Publishers, 1978), p. iii.

Chapter 10
1. Howard and Charlotte Clinebell, *The Intimate Marriage* (New York: Harper and Row, 1970), pp. 204, 211.
2. Dr. Sandra Candy, from a study reported in *Houston Post,* 17 March 1978.
3. Lauren Bacall, *By Myself* (New York: Knopf Publishing Co., 1978), p. 164.
4. Dr. James Dobson, *What Wives Wish Their Husbands Knew About Women* (Wheaton, IL: Tyndale House Publishers, 1975), p. 63.
5. Sidney Jourard, quoted in article by Carol Stacker, *Houston Post,* 17 March 1978.
6. Karen Burton Mains, *Open Heart, Open Home* (Elgin, IL: David C. Cook Publishing Co., 1976), p. 26.
7. Gerald Moore, "You Can't Do Without Other People," *Reader's Digest,* March 1978, p. 144.

Chapter 11
1. Dr. Mihaly Csikszentmihalyi, in *Psychology Today,* June 1976, p. 38.
2. Dr. Joyce Brothers, column in *Houston Post,* 8 January 1979.
3. "Gloria Peron, Queen of the Road," *Open Road and Professional Driver* magazine, February 1978, p. 8.
4. Howard Finch, Radio Station KTRH, Houston, TX.
5. Steve Berman, "Relationship," *New Marriage* magazine, quoted in article by Charlotte Phelan, *Houston Post,* 13 November 1978.
6. Karen Burton Mains, *Open Heart, Open Home* (Elgin, IL: David C. Cook Publishing Co., 1976), pp. 171–75.

Chapter 12
1. Henry A. Jordan, M.D. and Leonard S. Levitz, Ph.D., "How to Survive the Holidays," *Bon Appetit,* December 1977), p. 71.